HOLLYWOOD
Confidential

12 SECRETS TO BECOMING THE STAR OF YOUR OWN LIFE

STEVE JONES

HARPER
Celebrate

Published by Harper Celebrate, an imprint of HarperCollins Focus LLC.

Steve Jones is represented by Jennifer Smith of SPIN Literary

Art direction: Tiffany Forrester
Cover design: Micah Kandros
Cover photo: Uriel Sanchez
Interior design: Kristy Edwards

Any internet addresses (websites, blogs, etc.) in this book are offered as a resource. They are not intended in any way to be or imply an endorsement by HarperCollins Focus LLC, nor does HarperCollins Focus LLC vouch for the content of these sites for the life of this book.

Note: The contents and opinions of this book represent the practices and philosophies of the author, who has thoughtfully shared methodologies that have worked for him and stories from his personal experiences. Although these practices have also been successful among many other entertainers around the world, it's important to keep in mind that this book is meant to inspire and encourage, not be taken as a guarantee for success in the entertainment field.

ISBN 978-1-4002-4923-7 (HC)
ISBN 978-1-4002-4928-2 (audio)
ISBN 978-1-4002-4925-1 (epub)

Printed in Malaysia

25 26 27 28 29 30 PJM 7 6 5 4 3 2 1

THIS BOOK IS DEDICATED TO THE LOVING memory of my father, **Steve D. Jones**, a man whose rich legacy lives on within these pages, and deeply inside the four chambers of my heart. While the earthly untethering of your physical presence seems unbearable at times, spiritually, I feel you with me now more than ever. Thank you for using the rising tide of your life to lift my vessel.

CONTENTS

Foreword vii

Introduction xi

Secret #1: **C** OURAGE 1

Secret #2: **O** PTIMISM 27

Secret #3: **N** UANCE 43

Secret #4: **F** AITH 59

Secret #5: **I** NGENUITY 75

Secret #6: **D** ETACHMENT 91

Secret #7: **E** NDURANCE 107

Secret #8: **N** EGATIVITY 121

Secret #9: **T** ENACITY 137

Secret #10: **I** NTENTIONALITY 153

Secret #11: **A** UTHENTICITY 169

Secret #12: **L** UMINOSITY 185

Confidentially 200

Acknowledgments 204

Notes 207

About the Author 217

FOREWORD

I had no idea it was my destiny to become the first woman of color to play Cinderella. But I knew it was a transformative moment, not just for me and my career, but also for Black and brown girls around the world. That movie changed the way they saw and believed in themselves. So much so, that twenty-five years later, I still hear, "I believe I can be a princess because of you."

After selling more than sixteen million copies worldwide with my sophomore album, *Never Say Never*; winning the Grammy, along with Monica, for Best Performance by a Duo through our song, "The Boy Is Mine"; and being tapped as the first Black entertainer to secure a CoverGirl cosmetics contract, I had become one of the world's biggest stars. But with the recognition and achievement came pressure—pressure to remain relevant and to stay sitting on top of the world. Specifically, after the huge success of my TV show, *Moesha*, I started to feel trapped by my public "perfect image," and it caused me to question and be at war with myself.

As a result, I dealt with depression on and off for many years. At the height of my stardom, I was not the star of my own life, which is why I can't stress enough the importance of knowing who you are and being yourself. And if you don't know who you are . . . wait! It's not worth the risk of losing yourself. In retrospect, I am thankful for those hard times, as they truly helped me to tap into my full power. So, to anyone reading this who may be going through dark times in your life, know that you are equipped to handle it. Don't focus on what you are going through, but instead, focus on the light at the end of the tunnel. The tunnel is an illusion, and the light is what's real. And those are the types of teachings you'll learn in the pages to come.

To the reader who picked up this book wanting to become the star of your own life, you are off to a great start simply by recognizing there is more for you and seeking the knowledge to claim it. You have to know and believe there is a purpose for your life. You can start by figuring out what you're passionate about. What are your gifts and talents? What can you offer the world that only you can bring? Once you know what you've been called to do, like my friend Steve Jones, learn to let go and let purpose take its course. Then it will do just that, and you will be led in the right direction.

Through my journey, I have come to realize that who I am and always have been is a child of God. And it is a privilege to have access to the magic that is God, the same God who made the very heavens, earth, and stars in the universe. As human beings, it's our job to stay grounded and humble and to become a channel for God's creativity to flow through us. We are all vessels, allowing God to express himself through each of us. And in that way, it's never really about us; it's all about being a vessel.

Steve Jones is a vessel. And I can truly say that his purpose is to be used for something bigger than himself. He pours into all who encounter him, from celebrities to the stranger at the coffee shop.

In this book you will discover having a belief in God gave Steve the ability to see himself and where he wanted to be, only then to realize where he wanted to be is really where he actually was. We all have access to that. It's that faith that can take us anywhere we need or want to go. But we first must develop the discipline necessary to help us reach our goals. We all know that it's pretty much impossible to succeed without hard work. But I've found that the secret to working hard is in finding the love for what you do. Once you find it, you can push and motivate yourself to keep going, especially when "doing the work" feels overwhelming.

When it comes to my work, I have never been one to listen to criticism. Those who get it, get it. And those who don't? Those aren't my people. On your journey to becoming the star of your own life, I encourage you to find your people. Assemble a cast of stars who can cheer you on to greatness—ones who can remind you who you are when life causes you to question or doubt yourself. I am so blessed to have found Steve Jones. And now through this book, you have him too!

Brandy

INTRODUCTION

Picture it! It was 2019. There I was, on a rooftop in Hollywood, California, standing face-to-face with the world's biggest media mogul—Miss Oprah Winfrey. And it's not that I hadn't interacted with her before this, but this time I was standing before her as producer of the number one record-breaking docuseries on her network. Paparazzi lights were flashing, champagne was flowing, and the stars were aligning—illuminating the path to my next act.

With gratitude, I began to express my appreciation to Miss Winfrey for all she had done for my career, when she cut me off mid-sentence saying, "No need to thank me. You set an intention, and you did the work. You've created an entire love vertical within OWN programming. You're here because you did the work."

I knew this was my moment to expand my television portfolio—moving from producing to ideation. We snapped a picture together to commemorate the moment, and I shared my concept to produce a new special. She sent me to the president of the network and nine months later I had created, sold, and executive produced one of the top-rated specials of 2019, with appearances from Viola Davis and Tyler Perry and the first TV interview with Beyoncé in six long-awaited years. Not bad for my first project sold to a major network. I have since gone on to executive produce a number of projects for global conglomerates like Dove, Apple, Fox, and a host of entertainers, including Jennifer Lopez. We filmed her first holiday visual for a song she was featured on titled "It's the Most Wonderful Time of the Year" at the world-famous Grove here in Los Angeles.[1]

As Oprah affirmed, I have indeed done the work, accruing enough credits in my TV career to become an esteemed member of the Television Academy, the same institution that owns and operates the prestigious Emmys—the biggest night in television! And spiritually, I've been doing the work as well: healing, expanding, evolving, accepting, and loving myself. Setting and defending boundaries. Holding myself accountable and taking responsibility for the energy I bring into the room. You know, the work that really matters.

Today I work as a Hollywood producer living in the City of Angels, Los Angeles, California. But before I broke into the television space, I was—and still am—a bit of a "multi-hyphenate" (a fancy term for one who does *a lot*!). Over the years I've held many titles that include marketing executive, brand manager, content creator, and television producer. Some of my earliest jobs in Hollywood afforded me the opportunity to work on legendary studio lots like Paramount, Warner Brothers, and Sony Pictures, spearheading marketing campaigns for blockbuster films like *Creed*, starring Michael B. Jordan and Sylvester Stallone, and *Hateful Eight* by Quentin Tarantino, featuring Samuel L. Jackson.

As I continued to climb in my career, I ran into so many young dreamers who were lost or struggling on the path to pursuing their dreams. My first few years in Hollywood, I lent my couch and my wallet to fund the dreams of many, and a few of those couch surfers have gone on to win Oscars! Those early encounters helped to uncover a deep-seated desire in me to create space and opportunity for dreamers to dream, providing them with the tools they needed to succeed. As fate would have it, because of my passion for serving others, I bumped into one of the greatest versions of myself, earning me the title I'm *most* proud of: educator. At a time in my career when I had virtually no contacts, connections, or resources, I had the audacity to create Hollywood Confidential. It's a live-event series designed to teach dreamers how to break into the entertainment business through education, mentorship, and hands-on advice from one-on-one conversations with the most powerful voices and icons of color in entertainment. Some of the biggest names to hit our stage include internationally acclaimed filmmaker and Oscar-winning actress Lupita Nyong'o; fellow Academy Award-winning actress, director, and producer Regina King; Honorary Academy Award winner, and currently one of the highest-paid actresses in television, Angela Bassett; legendary lyricist and twenty-one-time Grammy-nominated first gentleman of hip-hop, Snoop Dogg; Golden Globe–nominated self-made serial entrepreneur, actress, and producer Issa Rae; and Emmy-winning influencer, actress, and "America's Mom," Tabitha Brown, to name a few.

Hollywood Confidential has been in existence for over a decade, from reaching hundreds of thousands of attendees in cities across the country, to receiving rave reviews in global publications. The series has served as a true North Star to those dreaming of a career in Hollywood. It has been my pleasure and honor to serve as a bridge between established and aspiring voices. What I didn't realize is that a simple idea I had to use the resources available to me to build a forum that served the aspiring Hollywood community would, in turn, also serve me, leading me into unlocking and achieving my wildest dreams. It is through Hollywood Confidential that I have learned an important lesson that guides me today: **Service breeds purpose.** I believe that discovering and living out our purpose is why we are all here on earth. It is our job to look within, to listen, and to discern our heart's song—allowing the lyrics and melody to lead us into our destinies.

As I looked back over my two-decades-long career in Hollywood, the countless stars I have interviewed, and the ones I have worked with on various productions, I began to see a pattern—a divine thread, if you will, weaving in and out of *their* various successes. As I moved among these legends, I began to discern the *secrets* to their successes. I wholeheartedly believe that through the examination of those who have achieved greatness, we can extract lessons and principles that can be applied to the road to our very own success.

But before you think this is another book glorifying celebrity, please know that's not what we're doing here. **Celebrity does not equal credibility.** Nor does it make celebrities any more important than the hardworking citizens who are the backbone of our economy. Echoing the sentiments of a mentor from afar, Marianne Williamson, I believe that we as a society are obsessed with stardom because we have not yet mastered becoming the stars of our own lives.

In the coming pages, I will seek to deconstruct the many excuses we hide behind and false narratives we cling to that hinder us from standing in the power of our own light. Together, we will grant ourselves permission to shine brightly and unapologetically as the stars we are all destined to be.

It takes a lot of bravery to cast ourselves as the lead in our own stories. Especially when circumstances and disappointments have conditioned us to believe that it's safer to move through our beautifully complicated lives

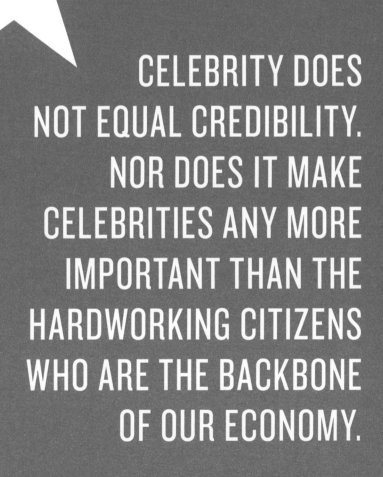

CELEBRITY DOES
NOT EQUAL CREDIBILITY.
NOR DOES IT MAKE
CELEBRITIES ANY MORE
IMPORTANT THAN THE
HARDWORKING CITIZENS
WHO ARE THE BACKBONE
OF OUR ECONOMY.

as background players or extras on the set of someone else's brightly lit stage. But I want to remind you that, just like the formation of the stars above, all of the components of your life—good and bad—have fused together to create one of the most unique and beautiful elements of the universe: you. And no matter what you've been through, you can rewrite your story, casting yourself as the victor, as opposed to being a victim of circumstance.

Today our world is giving way to an unprecedented awakening. The great equalizer, the events of 2020, came through like a wrecking ball, leveling the playing field and clearing the path for marginalized voices to rise to prominence. From the rise of Me Too and the Black Lives Matter movements, it's clear to me that now more than ever, it's time to come out of the shadows and speak our truths, boldly and unapologetically. Our stories, our experiences, and our shared perspectives are not only necessary but vital to the continued evolution of humanity.

With that in mind, I present to you *Hollywood Confidential*, a collection of twelve lessons I've learned from some of today's most powerful voices in entertainment. I'll be sharing with you what steps *they* took to turn their dreams into a reality and how you can apply their respective life lessons into transformative power for your own life. The reason I'm so excited to be on this journey with you is because I'm convinced that their unique experiences and stories of survival and triumph can teach you how to rise above obstacles to pursue your dream. On a deeper dive into this confidential material, you'll draw the strength and inspiration needed to pursue your passion and identify your purpose, ultimately bringing about true direction, inner peace, and a brighter outlook on life, regardless of vocation. Each chapter of *Hollywood Confidential* will inspire you to action, helping you harness and unlock your deepest potential whether you pursue a career in Hollywood or you take a different path to becoming the star of your very own life.

This project has been a labor of love for every person who has had a dream but may not have had the courage necessary to dream out loud. Perhaps you believe you waited too long to start. Or perhaps your dream has been derailed due to an unexpected interruption. But the very fact that we're still here lets us know that we have a purpose on earth yet to be fulfilled. Your dream may indeed be deferred, but not denied. And it may be that you are simply paralyzed by fear: fear of the unknown, fear of failure, or fear of not being enough. I want to affirm you in the reality that right now, in this moment, where you are, as you are, *you are more than enough*. You are more than enough. And you already possess everything you need to reach and achieve your dream. This collection of stories, including my own, is designed to inspire, uplift, and encourage you, serving as a blueprint to all of the possibilities that life has to offer you. I also hope it will equip you to become the greatest version of yourself.

One universal truth I live by is that you have the power to change the course of your life, simply by creating what you want to be part of. And you can absolutely manifest it. At the same time, what I refuse to do is sell you a pipe dream, painting a beautiful picture full of self-help mantras and false narratives to gas you up. The reality is that creating the life and career you want can be challenging, to say the least. Those who have broken into the industry or launched a global enterprise have experienced plenty of obstacles on their respective roads to success. The hard truth is that there *are* challenges and risks involved when it comes to following your dreams. But I'd rather you take that calculated risk in betting on yourself, instead of feeling unfulfilled at a nine-to-five job you never wanted to work in the first place, all the while knowing that your life is destined for greater.

If that speaks to you on any level, then this book was created with you in mind. Working with global icons and a myriad of dynamic entertainers has allowed me to accrue invaluable knowledge and experiences, which I've poured into this book. My goal is to help you pursue and achieve your wildest dreams, while unlocking the secrets to your very own personal success.

The purpose of this book is to serve *you*. It's meant to give you the tools and strategies that can equip you to fulfill that dream. This is a guide where you can learn the hard-won lessons from greats like Jennifer Lopez, Tyler Perry, Beyoncé, and Oprah Winfrey so that you can discover how to become the star of your very own life.

If you are ready to step into the greatest version of yourself, then let's do this. I'm sending you an abundance of love and support as you discover these twelve principles, which will equip you to become your best self and tap into your purpose on the world's stage as the star you were always meant to be.

NOTE: As you spend time with *Hollywood Confidential*, I'm encouraging you to have a journal nearby. Journaling is a meditative practice that helps us to stay present and practice mindfulness in written form. Throughout these chapters, and at the end of each one, I'll be suggesting exercises and practices that are tools to help you reflect *and act* on what you just discovered. Journaling allows us to take a deep spiritual inventory within our lives, providing us with critical information that guides us to our highest possibilities. I'm convinced that when you execute these journaling opportunities, you'll be better equipped to be the star of your own life.

NOTE: When I decided to take the risk to move from marketing to producing, I needed some extra gas in my tank. The messages I was hearing from myself, and those around me, caused me to question whether or not I could do it. And although we didn't have the appropriate language for it back then, I was suffering from imposter syndrome. After all, *who was I to think I could do something new*? The fuel I needed came by way of daily affirmations, which helped me to shift my thinking. So at the end of each chapter, I'll be offering you an affirmation you can post on your Instagram feed or your mirror, or use as a screensaver or tattoo on your heart. Each one is meant to give you what you need to succeed.

AFFIRMATION
for New Beginnings

I EMBRACE THE POWER OF NEW BEGINNINGS WITH AN open heart, understanding that change is a gateway to greater happiness. I am worthy of living a life of joy, purpose, and fulfillment. The doors of opportunity are now fully open to me, and my path is illuminated with the light of new possibilities. I release old storylines, narratives, and patterns that are holding me back. I have the power to create the life I truly deserve, and I fully give myself permission to shine and take my rightful place as the star of my own life.

Secret #1:
COURAGE

"I LEARNED THAT COURAGE WAS
NOT THE ABSENCE OF FEAR,
BUT THE TRIUMPH OVER IT. . . .
THE BRAVE MAN IS NOT HE WHO
DOES NOT FEEL AFRAID, BUT HE
WHO CONQUERS THAT FEAR."

—NELSON MANDELA

H ey Steve, I have bad news. The network believes it's a major conflict of interest for me to moderate your event. And if I do so, I could lose my job."

It was less than twenty-four hours before we were scheduled to launch our second installment of Hollywood Confidential, and the celebrity moderator I had secured pulled out of her commitment against her will. My heart was racing, and I began to panic at the thought of failing the thousands of hopefuls who'd be filling the venue with great expectation. Who would I get to moderate the event on such short notice?

"Don't worry," she assured me, "I found the perfect person to replace me!"

"Amazing, who is it?" I asked as I breathed a deep sigh of relief.

"It's you. You wrote the questions. You are the brainchild behind the event," she explained, "and it's time for you to stand in your power."

Trauma can be tricky. Often bidding us to do away with hidden dreams, desires, or versions of ourselves that we want to protect from rejection and the harsh realities of the world we live in. Up until this point in my career, I had prided myself on being behind the scenes. I told myself I was comfortable there, just outside of the spotlight's reach. The reality was, I had allowed fear and the opinions of others to cast me into the shadows. I truly believed that I hadn't achieved enough in my life or career to stand onstage alongside the greats. And by subscribing to that narrative, I was making a conscious decision to deny the greatness that lived inside of me.

With no other options and my back against the wall, I chose courage. I stepped onto the stage and into my light. Embracing the idea that I, too, was a star, I gave myself permission to shine. I grabbed that mic and moderated a conversation with ease and grace. It actually felt natural, as if I was born to do this! Now it's been ten years of moderating conversations, sitting across from some of the most fascinating and dynamic people of color in Hollywood, and I haven't given up that mic since.

So what does it truly mean to be the star of your own life? Simply put, it's having the bravery to prioritize the fulfillment of your dreams above all else. Allowing their fulfillment to become the North Star that guides every decision you make. It's emerging from the shadows of comfort, to take your rightful place at the center of your life's stage. And while that may sound easy, the reality is that it takes true courage to live the life you have always dreamed of. Especially when most of us are conditioned to minimize our deepest desires in the name of making a safer, more practical choice about our careers.

Here in Hollywood, when we say someone is a "star," not only does it mean that they've had a significant measure of professional success, but they also have a certain undeniable energy and presence, or a unique flair, that sets them apart from the rest. In my specific line of work as a producer, when someone is cast as the star of a TV production, it means they are a series regular, appearing at the center of each storyline. They're featured within the main credits as a principal actor. A step below the star of a TV show would be someone playing a recurring role, appearing in multiple episodes over the course of a season as the story demands. Next, we have guest stars, actors who appear in one episode, sometimes more, whose characters are often in multiple scenes and play a significant role in the story. Then we have co-stars, who support a scene or two with a small part, helping to move the story within that episode forward. Last, we have background actors, those who appear in the background of a scene in nonspeaking roles, helping to bring life to TV shows by making them look and feel authentic.

I wholeheartedly believe that many of us have been miscast in the wrong roles, operating as the background or as a supporting actor in the lives of others, when deep inside we know we're called to be the lead star in our very own story. We can be miscast by life's situation and circumstances, or by those who don't see our true worth and value. And then there are those of us who intentionally miscast ourselves to avoid the spotlight and the many pressures that come with standing before the world as our truest, most powerful selves. That type of fear-based thinking has prevented some of the greatest voices from rising to prominence, therefore robbing the world of so many gifts designed to enrich the lives of many. Les Brown, paraphrasing Myles Munroe, said it best when he stated, "The graveyard is the richest place on earth, because it is here that you will find all the hopes and dreams that were never fulfilled, the books that were never written, the songs that were never sung, the inventions that were never shared, the cures that were never discovered, all because someone was too afraid to take that first step, keep with the problem, or determined to carry out their dream."[1]

I believe we all have a divine mission to carry out while here on earth, and we are here for a limited time only. So why spend that time tortured by fear? We can instead cultivate a culture of courage deep within our hearts, allowing it to influence our decisions and how we show up in our own lives and in the lives of those we love.

Have you ever noticed how limitless children are when it comes to imagination and creativity? They have infinite freedom to express themselves, and most move through the world with such bravery and boldness. Jumping off the top of the monkey bars with no safety net? Sure, why not? Additionally, when you ask a five-year-old, "What do you want to be when you grow up?" they often respond with a myriad of exciting professions, from doctors and lawyers to professional athletes and entertainers, even astronauts! If you'd asked me what I wanted to be when I grew up, I would have announced, "Singer!" Children's imaginations can conceive the unlimited possibilities that life has to offer. Mostly because their ability to dream has not been crushed under the weight of the pressures of life. They haven't faced the pain of rejection. Their existence hasn't been invalidated. So when you were little, what did you want to become, before the world told you who you couldn't be?

I was raised in the small town of Warren, Ohio, about fifteen miles north of Youngstown, once the murder capital of the country. My father was an ambitious retail district manager who had grown up in the South, leaving behind his familial calling of sharecropping. And my mother was a schoolteacher who moonlit as a church evangelist on weekends. Being raised within a limited social construct, just a decade and some change out of the civil rights era, my life's trajectory—the one I was expected to live—was set and carved out for me pretty early on. And the entertainment industry was in no way deemed a viable option. But thankfully, representation matters.

Today—through the power of social media—the current generation of dreamers can see themselves represented on Instagram, YouTube, and

TikTok every day, and in every way. But that phenomena is relatively *new*. Back in the day all we had was "appointment" TV. *The Cosby Show* aired at 8 p.m. on Thursday night. There was no DVR and no streaming option. If you missed it, you missed it. My sister and I were latchkey kids: we came home from school and the TV was our babysitter while our dad was at work and our mom was putting herself through school to earn her bachelor's degree. Historically speaking, over the five decades that Americans had had televisions in their living rooms, there had been little cultural representation on television. But growing up in the 1990s, smack-dab in the middle of a televised Black renaissance, I was being shaped by shows like *A Different World, Living Single, Martin,* and *The Fresh Prince of Bel-Air.* Storytellers like Quincy Jones, Bill Cosby, and Yvette Lee Bowser were portraying the humanity and everyday living of African Americans *on-screen.* These nuanced depictions allowed me to see myself reflected in ways that caused me (and my world) to expand and inspired me to dream *bigger.*

As a matter of fact, the sole reason I went to college was because of *A Different World*—a *Cosby Show* spin-off, much of which was directed and produced by Debbie Allen, set in a historically Black college called Hillman. At the time, I had no idea it was a fictitious university, and you couldn't tell me that I wasn't enrolling in Hillman!

Becoming invested in the lives of the characters on the show expanded my world and opened my imagination up to all the possibilities therein. I wanted to build community with like-minded individuals in pursuit of our dreams. I wanted to hang out at "The Pit" cafeteria owned by Mr. Gaines (played by Lou Myers), who prepared meals for the students while being sure to dish an extra helping of TLC (Tender Loving Care).

I wanted to have a math teacher like Colonel Taylor aka "Dr. War" (played by Glynn Turman), whose tough-love tactics helped to ensure you didn't forget those lessons. And a dorm director like coach Walter Oaks (played by Sinbad), a gentle giant who made sure his residents were on the right track and in pursuit of their goals. (Instead, I got Cue Orr, who liked to party with his residents. But that's another story for another book!)

There were so many themes and lessons within the show that I was able to apply to my everyday life. Specifically, there was an episode way ahead of its time that helped me overcome the stigma surrounding therapy and mental health. Moving from behind the scenes to an on-camera role, Debbie Allen herself played the role of therapist Dr. Langhorne for one of the show's fan-favorite characters, Whitley Gilbert (played by Emmy-winning actress Jasmine Guy). Although a widely acceptable practice today, therapy was something once thought to be taboo in our society, especially among people of color. But imagine me, doing breathwork exercises and reciting positive mantras at just eleven years old. "Relax, Relate, Release!" Present day, on the side, I do a lot of work in the mental health space behind the scenes, and I credit my passion for that work to Debbie. Another episode that had a major impact on me tackled the LA riots, helping me to better address, identify, and unpack prejudice, implicit bias, and excessive force at the hands of the police. That episode opened a window from the Midwest into the city of Los Angeles—the good, the bad, and the ugly. Those early-on sneak peeks into West Coast culture helped me develop a love for the city I would one day occupy. Once again, representation matters. Seeing the work of Debbie Allen not only gave me a vision for who I could be, it also instilled in me the *courage* to believe I could achieve it.

As a teen I became an active participant in ushering in the digital age, moving from analog to digital with fervor and excitement. Napster's file-trading system had just launched, and Destiny's Child, the hottest girl group at the time, was gearing up to release their highly anticipated project *The Writing's on the Wall*. However, a full copy emerged on the internet months prior to the official release, thus becoming one of the first widely documented instances of digital piracy—soon to become a major threat to traditional album sales, changing the way we consumed music forever.

After first downloading the entire project (*smirk*), I looked up the phone number to Music World Management and demanded to speak to Mathew Knowles, father and then-manager of the group, which his daughter Beyoncé led. I explained to Mr. Knowles, who was not yet tech savvy, what was at stake with the situation. After assisting the team in removing the project from the internet, I was offered an internship opportunity as a digital brand moderator—a job that altered the trajectory that had been set for me, forever rerouting my own destiny.

In the wake of that early experience, I launched my first entertainment company while still in college. I didn't attend Hillman, but I did attend The Ohio State University, one of the largest universities in the world. There I organized a music-based event series called The Back to School Jam. I've always had a heart to give back, so even my first event series was free of charge. I brokered deals with Coca-Cola, Southwest Airlines, and a local cable TV network to cover the costs, allowing me to solely focus on creating events that fostered long-lasting, positive impact for communities of color. Because I've always had a desire to create opportunities for others, the proceeds from the events went toward creating mentoring and tutoring programs and scholarships to help African Americans graduate from OSU. (Go Bucks!)

After my career reached a proverbial glass ceiling in the Midwest, I packed up my life and abandoned every comfort I had ever known and headed out west! Talk about courage—it took plenty. Not to mention, my parents were not exactly in full support of my move. How much courage does it take to abandon your support system to go after your dream? It was a scary feeling because Ohio was all I'd known, and having to leave without the full blessing of my parents produced a level of fear that I had to work to push past. Whether you call it fear or anxiety, stress or discomfort, the feelings are typically the same. Oftentimes when we have a desire for change, we come face-to-face with fear of the unknown, which can keep us stuck or stagnant. But I knew that if I stayed in Ohio, my dreams would die, so I ventured to soil more conducive for my gifts to flourish, making California my new home.

I hit the ground running, picking up clients left and right! As I was representing talent on various marketing endeavors for monthly retainers, one of the first aspiring entertainers I ran into and befriended was Mr. Kendrick Sampson—who you may know from the Emmy Award–winning Shonda Rhimes show *How to Get Away with Murder*—a then-unknown Houston native who, like me, had driven across the country in pursuit of his big dream to become an actor. Through running lines with him for upcoming auditions, and transparent discussions on the challenges he faced while attempting to break into the industry, I developed a heart for the plight of actors, and in particular, actors of color. It's because of Kendrick and the passion and fearlessness he displayed in pursuit of *his* dream that I decided to move into marketing TV and film, and eventually created Hollywood Confidential. Kendrick is now not only known for *How to Get Away with Murder,* but also the Golden Globe–nominated HBO show *Insecure.* He's also starring as Quincy Jones in Lionsgate's upcoming Michael Jackson biopic and at the time of writing this just announced a role opposite Al Pacino!

After being in Los Angeles for about six years, I eventually worked my way up to marketing my first huge theatrical release, *Creed.* The film starred legendary actor Sylvester Stallone and *future* legend Michael B. Jordan. His meteoric rise to superstardom has been a sight to witness and an inspiration to many. Michael grew up in the tough streets of Newark, New Jersey, with dreams and aspirations of breaking into the entertainment industry. At age eleven, a visit with his mother to his mother's doctor's office brought about the affirmation he needed to pursue his dreams. The receptionist, whose children were working models, took one look at him and told his mother that she should sign him up for modeling without delay. Soon after, his modeling career began, landing print campaigns for Toys "R" Us.

Jordan worked his way up from print campaigns to a prominent role in the Keanu Reeves movie *Hardball,* after which he landed a breakout role in the Emmy-nominated, critically acclaimed HBO series *The Wire,* starring as Wallace, a sixteen-year-old drug dealer. That role put him in a position to receive an influx of opportunities he had dreamed of. He ended up taking on a full-time role on the ABC soap opera *All My Children* as the troubled teen Reggie Montgomery. After three seasons on the soap, Jordan decided to pivot.

Jordan desired to express himself outside of the confines of the stereotypical street thug role commonly available to male African

American actors. With hallmark *courage*, he approached his agent about diversifying his on-screen opportunities, opting to strive for roles that were written for men of *any* race, instead of roles crafted for Black men only. What made that a risk was the fact that he'd be excluding himself from so many of the roles that *were* available at the time. Soon came roles that gave him the opportunity to show true versatility, range, and depth, in movies like *Red Tails* and *Chronicle* and the popular TV show *Friday Night Lights*. As fate would have it, the success of those projects brought Jordan face-to-face with his life-changing role: Oscar Grant in *Fruitvale Station* (2013), written and directed by Ryan Coogler—Jordan's first leading role in a feature film. The film became an indie hit, with rave reviews for Coogler's ability to masterfully weave together topical narratives with racial themes. Jordan also received praise and critical acclaim for his performance. The success of the film not only placed Jordan in the spotlight but also helped him develop a passion for being part of content that makes the African American community proud. Jordan explained to *GQ*, "We don't have black mythologies and folklore that's on the big screen and small screen, period. . . . I want to help bring those to the masses, the same stories, bedtime stories, that I was being told."[2] The success of *Fruitvale* also set Jordan up to star in the film *Creed*, where we met.

As a marketer, working with studios to come up with campaigns to promote their films can be exciting but also *challenging*, especially when working the African American promotional campaign and attempting to explain our culture to studio heads, shareholders, and decision makers who aren't Black.

I had a succession of challenges implementing well-conceived strategies and concepts for the film. At times, it was as if the decision makers (who are no longer employed there) wanted me to accept the premise that African American audiences were a monolith, and that my campaign's ideas should be watered down to cater to who they believed the African American demographic to be. My ideas were stripped and replaced with ideas of what they *thought* would attract African American audiences, based on stereotypes, generalizations, and assumptions. Even still, the film did well, bringing in over forty-two million for the five-day Thanksgiving weekend. Doors were flying open for me to continue working box office projects, but my history with studio execs and their inability to understand the rich and vast culture of African American audiences left a bad taste in my mouth. I no longer wanted to continue in marketing, as I couldn't see myself fighting to explain myself to people who had already committed to misunderstanding my culture for the duration of my career in entertainment.

Just like Michael before me, I knew it was time to make a pivot in my career. I believed in my heart that the power was no longer in marketing stories, but in *creating and producing* the content to make long-lasting positive change. I knew it would take sheer courage to reinvent myself, moving from a marketer to a producer. And although the skillsets are definitely transferable, starting over in a new career without a proven track record is not advised. Especially when the bills are due. But I had to follow the calling within my heart.

I don't know how it works for you, but oftentimes once I make a decision to stand firm on a certain principle or way of living, life has a way of challenging or calling me out on said decision, just to make sure I really mean it. Not even six months after deciding to leave marketing, I was approached to do the marketing for a new and at the time unnamed docuseries that celebrated marriage in the African American community.

Although tempted, I immediately responded to the offer by announcing, "I no longer do marketing, but for a producer credit, I can help shape the show, while offering marketing consulting on the side."

It worked!

That show ended up being called *Black Love*, which was picked up for distribution on OWN, the Oprah Winfrey Network, where it became the biggest unscripted debut in her network's history! Courage carried me through to my next act.

I believe that our lives will shrink or expand in direct proportion to the level of courage we possess. Staying in a space we have outgrown reduces our quality of living. Why be a prisoner to fear when we can live in freedom? I want courage to stretch out inside of me to the extent that it permeates throughout every area of my life, giving others a tangible example of what it means to be courageous—even if it means doing it afraid. That's why I created Hollywood Confidential, a destination for dreamers who want to move into action.

When it comes to pursuing our dreams, we are oftentimes plagued by fear, which we mask as excuses. Sometimes we even have a fear of success itself. Instead of giving into fear, what if we chose love, by choosing ourselves? What if we all went after our dreams, boldly, and without reservation?

To the unfulfilled housewife, high school student, overwhelmed single mother, or the newly married husband trying his hand at building a legacy, I ask you, What was your dream? No, really, close your eyes, and return to that childlike state where you could be and do anything. Before life became all too real, full of challenges and obstacles. What did you want to be, and what stopped you from following your dream? Today is the day that you start to reclaim your dream.

THE SIX REASONS PEOPLE DON'T FOLLOW THEIR DREAMS

In sitting down with so many young dreamers over the last decade, many of whom gave up just before realizing their dreams, I began to notice a few themes or deterrents that held them back from fully pursuing the lives they wanted to live, and I wanted to share them with you.

FEAR OF FAILURE

When we utilize logic to make decisions that don't force us to rely on courage, those decisions are often rooted in fear, requiring minimal risk and producing minimal results. Of course, none of us want to fail. But no person who has achieved greatness did so without challenges, roadblocks, and bouts of extreme failure along the way. We must have the courage to take the first step, believing that when we do, the path will be made clear.

FEAR OF CHANGE

A quote (actually a Thoreau misquote) that has always motivated me to live out loud and in purpose—on purpose—says, "Most men lead lives of quiet desperation."[3] Many choose to move through life empty and unfulfilled, which can be directly attributed to fear of change. It's easier to live within the shadows of mediocrity than to risk going after a dream that seems bigger than you. We must learn to embrace and transform our fears, repurposing them as fuel in the tank of progress and change.

PRIORITIES

The prioritization of our dreams is key to becoming the star of our own lives. Yes, we all have responsibilities. However, the deprioritization of our purpose—to cater to the needs of everyone else—is a slippery slope that ends in unfulfillment. I'm in no way asking you to be selfish, but I am asking you to get comfortable with placing your dreams first, casting yourself as the lead role within your story, to ensure the best possible conclusion before the final credits of your life role.

LACK OF CONFIDENCE

Placing yourself on the center stage within the spotlight takes absolute bravery and courage. It can be intimidating and cause you to doubt yourself, your gifts, and your abilities. Those are the times when imposter syndrome demands, "Who do you think you are to boldly go after your dreams?" If that's you, allow me to remind you that you were born worthy, and inside of you resides every single thing you need to be successful. So take the risk! I'd rather you fail than live the rest of your life never knowing what would have happened if you'd only had the confidence to be courageous.

TIMING

Can I just tell you that there will never be a perfect time to go after your dream? As a matter of fact, there will never be a perfect time to go after anything. And in waiting for the perfect time, we allow life to pass us by. All we have is now, and now is in fact the best time to seize the moment and make the most out of every opportunity.

LACK OF SUPPORT

Frequently, those closest to you can unknowingly project their own fear of failure onto your dreams, serving as a deterrent to achieving your life's true purpose. The people you know and love may not be the ones cheering the loudest for your success. Most times, your biggest expressions of support will come from perfect strangers, as many peers can't handle the fact that you've decided to push past their perceived limits and societal norms to achieve greatness. And that is why it's important to follow the compass of your own heart above the opinions, feelings, and thoughts of others—including those closest to you.

Can you relate to any of the aforementioned dream killers? If so, I have news for you: *we all go through it.* If you're like most people, you probably relate courage with fearlessness, but that's an incorrect comparison. Courage is moving forward in spite of the fear you may feel. Courage means ignoring the fear that may be tugging away at you and pressing on. One of the most effective ways to be courageous is to recognize what you're afraid of and refuse to allow fear to paralyze you. Being courageous allows you to take chances, pursue your dreams, and get what you want out of life.

If you've been struggling with fear and want to feel more courageous in your life, I'm going to offer you some tips that will show you how to tap into your courage. It takes work to move beyond your fears. The more you are able to face your fears, the more you will replace your fear-based responses with courageous ones.

A new acronym for courage that I have constructed to help me stay motivated is as follows:

C HALLENGES
O FTEN
U NVEIL
R EMARKABLY
A CCELERATED
G ROWTH
E XPERIENCES

A true agent of social change and champion of courage, Michael B. Jordan has leveraged his cachet in Hollywood to shine a light on marginalized stories and amplify underrepresented voices through his production banner, Outlier Society. This venture allows Jordan to sit at the helm of each project, offering creative input from inception to completion. Additionally, he's unveiled his Black-owned and Black-led marketing agency, Obsidianworks, which bridges the gap between companies and the consumer to encourage authentic representation of people of color.

And myself? I'm doing pretty good as well. Hollywood Confidential will be partnering with Meta's Culture and Content Equity team and their marquee programs for creatives of color—We the Culture and Dale Tú—to empower the next generation of diverse storytellers, actors, writers, and producers via custom education, programming, events, and grants that match aspiring creatives to industry titans.

For the last three years, we've been nurturing our relationship with Meta's Head of Culture and Content Equity, Michelle Mitchell, to support marginalized and underrepresented voices. We want to create content that allows people of color to see themselves reflected in ways that inspire them to become their best selves and empowers them to take actionable steps to achieve their creative dreams. The first drumbeat of this meaningful partnership was heard at Hollywood Confidential's 10th Anniversary in October, 2023.

Being courageous truly pays off in unimaginable ways.

We all have a divine mission to carry out while here on earth and we're here for a limited time only. So why spend that time tortured by fear when we can instead cultivate a culture of courage deep within our hearts?

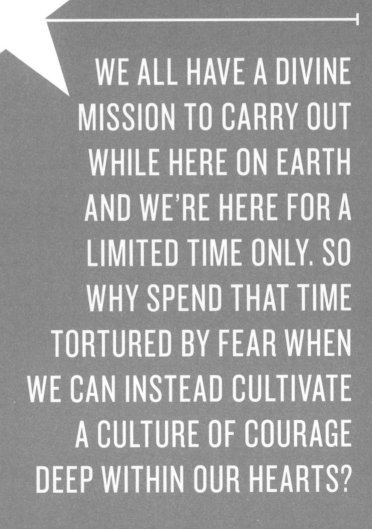

WE ALL HAVE A DIVINE
MISSION TO CARRY OUT
WHILE HERE ON EARTH
AND WE'RE HERE FOR A
LIMITED TIME ONLY. SO
WHY SPEND THAT TIME
TORTURED BY FEAR WHEN
WE CAN INSTEAD CULTIVATE
A CULTURE OF COURAGE
DEEP WITHIN OUR HEARTS?

SIX STEPS

TO APPLY THE SECRET OF *COURAGE* TO YOUR LIFE

FACE YOUR FEARS

Write down all the things you fear about pursuing your dream, and share, with a friend you trust, your commitment to facing these fears. When we commit to confronting what scares us, we can evolve into a more bold, confident, and courageous human being.

IDENTIFY YOUR STRENGTHS

Create a list of your gifts, skills, talents, and abilities. Knowing what you're good at will raise your confidence, which makes it easier to take risks and be courageous. When you're confident in your skillset and abilities, you'll find yourself rising to each and every occasion when opportunity presents itself.

CELEBRATE COURAGEOUS ACTIONS

Because every courageous moment should be celebrated, I want you to recall when you've acted with courage in the past despite feeling fearful. It's important to pat yourself on the back and recognize the strength it took to face your fears.

WELCOME FAILURE

Failure is often the key ingredient to success. With the right perspective, our failures should simply push us into solutions, fueling our determination and our resolve. While failure does not guarantee success, the lessons extracted can be used as tools that help us build the life of our dreams. Pause to recall the times that you have failed, and beside each one note the lesson you learned from it.

CREATE ACCOUNTABILITY

Identify people in your life you can truly be vulnerable with about your fears. Call or text each one to let them know you need them. Those people will then serve as points of accountability, helping you to make true progress in leading a more courageous life.

DO IT AFRAID

Don't let fear stifle your dreams. Put one foot in front of the other, and push past your perceived limitations. Believe that everything you have ever dreamed of can be found on the other side of fear. This week, choose one of the fears you listed in the first exercise and take the first step to move toward your dream *despite that fear.*

QUESTIONS
for Reflection

What is the role in which I've cast myself? Is it truly the role I'm meant to play? Why or why not?

What did I want to become in adulthood, when I was a child? What did I want to become, before the world told me who I couldn't be?

How has fear shown up in my life and how has it impeded me from reaching my goals?

What are my limiting beliefs that hinder me from living a fully courageous life?

In what areas of my life can I be more courageous?

AFFIRMATION
for Courage

I AM A WARRIOR, AND MY COURAGE IS A SWORD THAT helps me slay the dragons of fear occupying space in my life. I have the strength to overcome perceived limitations, and I boldly face all obstacles that impede my progress. My dreams are much more valid than any fears I may harbor. I am moving into action and pursuing my aspirations while allowing the courage of my heart to dissolve all fear, doubt, and worry.

Secret # 2:
OPTIMISM

"THE POSITIVE THINKER SEES

THE INVISIBLE, FEELS THE

INTANGIBLE, AND ACHIEVES

THE IMPOSSIBLE."

—WINSTON CHURCHILL

ack in 2006, Rhonda Byrne published a massively success-ful book called *The Secret*, which resonated with readers all around the world. The book focused on the Law of Attraction, suggesting that thoughts and emotions are forms of energy and have a significant influence on our realities. Those who maintain an optimistic mindset will draw positive outcomes and manifest their deepest desires—while attracting suc-cess in all areas of their lives. Meanwhile, those who maintain a negative mindset will receive a barrage of negative outcomes. Seems pretty simple, right? So, around that time, I started to lean into the teachings of *The Secret,* and even found myself praying and asking for opportunities to practice positive thinking. I hadn't calculated that, in order to do so, I would be met head-on with negative situations that carried the potential to derail my hopes and dreams.

Sometime after I'd read *The Secret,* I pitched a TV show to the man-agement team of one of my favorite entertainers. After not hearing back for some time, I discovered that the entertainer and their team developed their own variant of the concept, pitched the show, and sold the concept to a network, void of my participation.

You would have thought my entire world had come to an end.

Depression hit me like a ton of bricks. I was angry, I was bitter, I was full of resentment—so much so, I considered leaving the entertainment business altogether. I gave up. While planning my exit strategy, I received a life-altering message from an earth angel by the name of Marianne Williamson. I happened to be watching an interview with Williamson, when I heard her say, "You can have a grievance, or a miracle; but you cannot have both."[1] Those words rocked me to my core. Of those two, I knew which I wanted.

After releasing the hurt and offense, I chose to embrace the power of positive thinking. For the first time ever, I created a vision board that consisted of all of the wonderful things I wanted to manifest in my life. At the top of that vision board, I designed a cover for a book titled *Hollywood Confidential,* setting my supreme intentions of obtaining a book deal. And not just with any publisher, but with HarperCollins. This, my friends, is how I know beyond the shadow of any doubt the power of optimism. **A positive mindset is the hallmark of creativity and the bridge to accomplishing our dreams.**

How about you? Are you an optimist or a pessimist? Is the glass half empty or is it half full? That's the age-old question. It's been said that a pessimist sees the difficulty in every opportunity, and an optimist sees the opportunity in every difficulty. My definition of optimism can be summed up as a belief or hope that the outcome of a specific endeavor, or outcomes in general, will be positive, favorable, and desirable.

Growing up, I can remember encountering eternal optimists and wondering if they were born that way or if they had to work at it like I do. I'll admit that my natural way of thinking has, historically, aligned more with pessimism—as a precautionary measure. Oftentimes, when we experience traumatic events, we can develop defense mechanisms and patterns of thinking to prevent ourselves from reliving or reexperiencing that which has historically hurt us and brought us pain.

A game changer for me was in learning to reframe my way of thinking, centering myself inside the belief system that goodness can be found in every situation, including those that are incredibly bad. As a result, I believe that each one of us can opt for optimism. Optimism is a choice, and a muscle that can be developed within the recesses of even the most critical of minds.

Growing up in the late 1990s, at the height of MTV's popularity, I developed a deep love for R & B music. Whitney, Michael, Janet, Mariah, Usher, D'Angelo, and a host of other innovative artists were in their prime. And then there was Brandy—the teenage multi-talent (singer, actor, and dancer) who scored a succession of history-making firsts through the power of positive thinking and believing in her dreams.

At four years old, Brandy relocated with her family to Los Angeles from McComb, Mississippi, to break into the industry and reach her very specific dreams. She recalled, "I had three dreams: to be a star, have a band, and to meet Whitney Houston."[2] But she did so much more than that.

In September 1994, when she was fifteen, Brandy's debut self-titled album sold over six million copies worldwide, fueled by lead singles "Baby," "Best Friend," "Brokenhearted," and "I Wanna Be Down." The success of that project allowed her to star in her own prime-time series, *Moesha*, for six seasons. This path set the stage for Brandy to be hand-selected by her soon-to-be fairy godmother, Whitney Houston, to star opposite her as Cinderella in the 1997 musical film by the same name—making her the first Black actress to ever portray the character on-screen. How's that for the power of positive thinking?

In fact, Brandy was in such high demand that Mattel approached her about creating the Brandy Doll. "We picked Brandy because she shows girls that they can do anything," said a Mattel spokesperson. "As a successful singer and actress, she is inspirational."[3] Additionally, she starred in other memorable roles in blockbuster franchise films like *I Still Know What You Did Last Summer*, opposite Jennifer Love Hewitt, and *Double Platinum*, opposite Diana Ross. To date, Brandy has sold over forty million records worldwide, cementing her place in American music history as one of the bestselling female artists of all time.

Brandy's early success definitely spoke to the young dreamer inside of me. Her achievements served as a master class full of lessons on believing in yourself, your dreams, and the power of manifestation through positive thinking. My first childhood crush, only rivaled by Aaliyah, the first cassette tape I ever purchased after mowing lawns all summer long, and the first time I can truly say I fell in love with music can all be credited to Brandy Norwood. Watching Moesha and her friends walk the corridors of Crenshaw High not only provided a window into the culture of Southern California living, but also taught me invaluable coming-of-age lessons that I wasn't quite learning in the real world. And that's the power of good television. It can be used as a medium of mass communication, providing educational tools and promoting a strong sense of morals and values in the lives of viewers around the world, ultimately helping to shape society.

After the pilot episode of *Moesha* aired, I definitely *"want(ed) to be down!"* In my mind, you couldn't tell me that we wouldn't one day be friends. I knew our paths were destined to cross, and sure enough, I ended up sitting right behind her at a music concert one random night.

That's just the magic of Los Angeles. Brandy is known as the Vocal Bible due to her distinctive tone, complex harmonies, soothing melodies, and pristine vocal acrobatics, and I knew that if I hit the perfect musical riff or run just right, I could get her attention. So that's what I did. Sure enough, she turned around and said, "Oh my God, that run!" to which I responded, "I learned from the best!" And that was the beginning of a lifelong friendship.

Befriending a legend is hard! Or at least it was for me. Here I am, hanging out with the famous girl from inside the TV, known and loved all around the world by millions of fans as a *true* vocalist and your favorite singer's singer. This was also the girl whose posters hung in my middle school locker? *Bruh!* Mind blowing. But my inability to differentiate between the girl I loved on TV and the one before me in real life served as a hindrance to our potential friendship. One day, in sheer frustration regarding my inability to be fully myself around her, she looked me in the eye and said, "Stop treating me like Brandy!" And that was our breakthrough. From that day forward, we've been able to build a true friendship rooted in our shared experiences of humanity, not the accolades, achievements, or fame.

Brandy has become my very own personal alchemist, teaching me how to transmute pessimistic thoughts into optimism. For one of my birthdays, after I expressed difficulty maintaining optimism about reaching my dreams, Brandy gifted me a beautiful, sturdy leather journal with a yellow satin ribbon for keeping my place. She explained the value to me, saying, "I've been doing 'morning pages,' a daily practice first thing each morning in my journal. It helps to get the negative thoughts out, making space for positivity and creativity to thrive." And there began my long-standing relationship with journaling. It truly has helped me to harness and process my thoughts and transform my dreams into reality. There is a discipline in journaling that helps the mind become a breeding place for miracles. Writing out my vision and later being able to revisit the things that have manifested has helped me to remain positive in the face of adversity, knowing that everything always works out for my highest good.

A loyal and dependable friend I can always count on, Brandy became one of the first big celebrities to sit down for an interview with Hollywood Confidential, helping to legitimize and popularize the brand. The epitome of optimism, she spoke openly during the interview on the importance of dreaming and believing in yourself. "God gives you your dreams," she said, "and you have to believe that He has the power to accomplish those dreams through you." She continued, "With life comes up and downs, and we have to learn to adjust. I've had my share of dark moments, but those are the times where my bond was created with God. To anyone out there pursuing your dreams and your purpose, know that you have to stay strong, and don't be afraid to ask for guidance, and clarity. You have to believe in yourself, and above all you have to keep going, because too many of us give up just before we reach the promise."[4]

And we can see from Brandy's life what happens if you never give up on yourself. From being one of the first African Americans to star as Roxie Hart in the legendary Broadway musical *Chicago*, to receiving her star on the Hollywood Walk of Fame for her groundbreaking achievements and contributions to the entertainment community, Brandy's belief in herself not only allowed her to fulfill her dreams, but also helped to inspire new dreams and possibilities in the lives of millions around the world. She absolutely has inspired me.

Before I met Brandy, before I even moved to LA, on every visit to the city I'd find my way to The Grove, my favorite entertainment complex in the city. They have a large central park with an animated fountain that makes me feel like I am in an Italian village. It's my European excursion right in the middle of central Los Angeles. Movies, shopping, and fine dining all set to the soundtrack of big band music from the 1930s. It's a whole *vibe*. I could be there for hours, people-watching. Since it's located right next door to CBS Studios, I'd see Tyra Banks, shopping after filming *America's Next Top Model*. For me, it became the place where I would dream. I'd imagine what might be awaiting me in Los Angeles. I'd vision-cast and consider what might be. I think there was just a magic, an energy, that drew me to that location. It's where I could be optimistic about a future I couldn't yet see. When I moved to the city, I'd continue to visit The Grove, but I also expanded my spaces to dream to include Mulholland Drive and the Universal City Overlook, situated above the entire city with those breathtaking panoramic views. They became my sacred places where I would re-encounter my dreamer within, full of optimism and awe. It's where I encounter my younger self and reflect on where my optimism has brought me and where I can, once more, dream with optimism for the future.

What's that safe and sacred place for you? Close this book, grab your journal, and begin thinking about the role that the secret of optimism may be playing in your journey. Maybe, like Brandy, you're a natural optimist. (If so, you've checked the box.) But maybe you've suffered a blow, a disappointment, or a setback, as I did when my show idea was stolen, and you need to *choose* optimism. Whatever the case, be open to welcoming new possibilities. I encourage you to make the choice *for* optimism.

This second secret to becoming the star of your own life has truly been my saving grace. Having actively worked toward optimism, allow me to share five quick ways you can train your mind to believe and attract the best that life has to offer.

FIVE STEPS

TO APPLY THE SECRET OF *OPTIMISM* TO YOUR LIFE

SILENCE YOUR INNER CRITIC

Our inner dialogue has the ability to propel or imprison us. At times, we can become our own worst critics, allowing our negative thoughts and reviews on our life stories to drive us into destructive behavior. We must instead practice balance, challenging our inner critic with facts that we know to be true of ourselves. Begin to develop the practice of capturing these negative thoughts in your journal, in one column, and in a second column write down what is *more true* than the voice of your internal critic.

REFRAME YOUR THINKING

Reframing is one of the most powerful tools we have. It helps us to shift our mindset, turning negative thoughts into opportunities for change and growth. The frame through which we view a situation determines our point of view and our perception of situations and experiences. When the frame is shifted, the meaning changes, thereby changing our mindset and behaviors. This week, when you find yourself in a negative situation, open your journal and reframe your thoughts, training your mind to find the good in everything.

HAVE AN ATTITUDE OF GRATITUDE

If you're having trouble leaning into the power of optimism, may I suggest that you begin to view the world through a lens of gratitude?

Gratitude is the practice of acknowledging and appreciating the good things in your life, whether big or small. It completely changes the way we see the world, and ourselves in it. When we choose gratitude, we are choosing to live a life rooted in positivity, for, in the words of Michael J. Fox, "With gratitude, optimism becomes sustainable."[5] Use a page of your journal to make a list of everything you can be grateful for.

POSITIVE REINFORCEMENT

Remaining in a perpetual state of optimism is possible through positive reinforcement. What I mean by that is, when you notice yourself creating new patterns of positivity where the old you never would have, reward yourself. Pat yourself on the back. By acknowledging your progress and just how far you have come, you help to reinforce these healthy patterns, increasing the probability that they will reoccur.

SURROUND YOURSELF WITH POSITIVE PEOPLE

While working toward becoming a more positive person, monitoring the company you keep becomes essential. The harsh reality is one bad apple can indeed spoil the whole barrel. Don't be afraid to recast relationships to ensure a positive experience and outcome in the story of your life. Reflect, in your journal, about the people who are and are not positive "apples" in your life.

QUESTIONS
for Reflection

What are the disappointments I'm harboring that could be hindering me from maximizing my life's purpose?

How am I allowing the voice of my inner critic to drown out the positives that I know to be true about myself?

What are the ways in which my current pattern of thinking is allowing me to manifest myself as the star of my own life?

In what ways can I safeguard my dreams and goals from pessimism?

What changes can I make to ensure that my life leans more into optimism?

AFFIRMATION
for Optimism

MY MIND IS A MAGNET, AND I CHOOSE TO ATTRACT positive things into my life by thinking positive thoughts. I have the power to reframe my way of thinking, aligning myself with the best options that life has to offer. Never empty, my cup continues to overflow with happiness, peace, and joy. I choose to see the positive in every facet of life, including those within myself.

Secret # 3 :
NUANCE

"THE MOON PUTS ON AN ELEGANT
SHOW, DIFFERENT EVERY TIME IN
SHAPE, COLOUR, AND NUANCE."

—ARTHUR SMITH

Today, I proudly identify as "multi-hyphenate." But that wasn't always the case. As I shared, I was originally a marketer, who could position the product, devise a strategy, produce content, and attach a brand. And I could also sing on the side? *Nah.* That felt like a lot. I can remember being in the studio with multiplatinum-selling, Grammy Award–winning clients, terrified to hum a bar out of concern that I'd be thought to have a hidden agenda. I feared they would see me posing behind a video camera with secret ambitions of becoming a signed recording artist. Whether or not that was how they saw me, being perceived as a jack of all trades and master of none was my biggest fear. So, I opted to lead with just one of those gifts, denying myself the opportunity to be fully expressed. That was one of the biggest mistakes in my career. If I could do it all over again, I'd be less concerned with the perceptions of others and more concerned with the fulfillment of my soul's purpose and the things that make me happy. The good news is, there's still time!

If I could offer any advice to you on your path to success, it would be to give yourself permission to be every single thing that you can be, refusing to bury any parts of yourself, while being sure to use all the crayons in your coloring box. I understand and respect the line of thinking behind homing in on one particular gift and committing to perfecting it. But I'm going to give you permission to do the exact opposite. We are all multidimensional human beings, with many aspects and facets that make us who we individually are. And each of those aspects of who we are deserves to be seen and celebrated. When we embrace and honor the variety of those unique and special elements, we embrace the power of nuance. And that's a superpower.

I want to encourage you to live a *nuanced* life. If someone or something is nuanced, the person or object has multiple characteristics or layers of meaning that can't easily be categorized. Nuance resists stereotype. I have always believed that nuance serves as a major point of differentiation that sets you apart from your "competition" every time. I use quotation marks around the word because I believe there is no such thing as competition, as what's yours is yours, engraved and gold-plated with your name on it. Nobody can take that away. The only person who can impede your purpose is you. And the only person you should be competing with is who you were yesterday.

Remember, having unique gifts, talents, and abilities that cause you to stand out from the crowd is your *superpower*. Lean into what makes you different, special, and unique. A differentiated presence in any field is *key* for maximum visibility and optimal success. Being able to hone multiple talents amplifies your presence and impact, and makes you a true force to be reckoned with.

Don't believe me? Look at triple threat Jennifer Lopez, a dancer, singer, and actress whose movies have grossed over one billion dollars at the box office worldwide. Jennifer's journey is a testimony to the power of nuance when you have more than one unique gift and are willing to pivot.

Growing up in the Bronx, Jennifer dreamed of one day making it big in the entertainment industry. There was always music, dancing, laughter, and a lot of love in her family's home. After expressing her desire to become a famous actress, her family was surprisingly unsupportive—mostly because at that time, there weren't any famous Latinas to serve as a tangible paradigm for success.

Remember the impact that watching *A Different World* had on me? It put me on the path to pursuing higher education. Jennifer's experience is just another reason we so desperately need nuanced representation in TV and film. How can we be what we don't see? Jennifer's disagreement with her parents over pursuing entertainment instead of completing her college degree led her to move out of her home and figure out how to survive on her own. Jennifer slept on the floor of quite a few dance studios in pursuit of her dream, as many starving artists do. After performing as a background dancer on spot dates and several worldwide tours, alongside appearing in a number of music videos, her hard work and sacrifice finally paid off. With a relocation to Los Angeles, she landed her first full-time professional dance job on the comedy sketch show *In Living Color*. Created by Keenan Ivory Wayans, it featured then-unknown stars Jamie Foxx, Chris Rock, and Jim Carrey.

After landing a few supporting roles, Jennifer's big break in acting came from starring as the widely celebrated Queen of Tejano Music, Selena, in the movie of the same name. The movie was a huge box office success, and Lopez became the first Latina actress to earn one million dollars for a film. But instead of continuing down the path she blazed in cinema, she made a bold and unexpected decision to follow her heart and pursue a career in music.

Her debut project *On the 6* was certified triple platinum, fueled by the No. 1 Billboard chart-topping single "If You Had My Love."[1] Her calculated risk paid off! Lopez is one of the ten most successful women in the history of music,[2] selling over eighty million records worldwide, accumulating fifteen billion music streams and eighteen billion music video views.[3] And if you thought the nuance of J.Lo stops at being a singer, actress, and dancer, you thought wrong. She's also a producer with her own company, Nuyorican Productions, an entrepreneur with her skincare line, JLo Beauty, and an advocate for Latinx communities through her philanthropic organization Limitless Labs, which is coordinating with other firms to invest fourteen billion dollars in Latina-owned businesses by 2030.[4]

I had the pleasure of first working with Jennifer in 2020, when I received a call to secure funding for a music video she was to be featured in alongside famed vocal coach Stevie Mackey. The song was a remake of the 1963 Christmas classic "It's the Most Wonderful Time of the Year" by Andy Williams. I had a week to make a miracle happen, but I knew with God, all things were possible, and there was no way I was going to turn the opportunity down to work with Selenasssssss! (Anything for her!) A dear friend of mine, Carla, connected me with the Cadillac brand, where I pitched placing one of their vehicles in the music video for a product integration play. The pitch landed, and I became the sole funder of the music video, in exchange for an executive producer credit. And to sweeten the deal, the music video was shot at the world-famous Grove in Los Angeles—the same spot where twelve years prior, I daydreamed about my future Hollywood career. Talk about a beautiful full-circle moment.

I was fortunate enough to team up with Jennifer again in 2021.

I received a call from *Adweek*—one of the largest, most respected marketing and media conglomerates in the business.

They reached out looking for me to secure an honoree for their Brand Visionary award. After mentioning some of the biggest names in the industry (and I do mean the biggest), I unexpectedly found myself saying, "If this is about branding, and we know that branding is about getting your target demographic to view you as one of the leading authorities in your field through consistently delivering a promise, then I prefer Jennifer Lopez. No one has been more consistent in delivering a promise than J.Lo. And clearly, her promise has resonated. She's dominated the world of pop culture in every facet. She's who I prefer for this opportunity."

As the project unfolded, I was afforded the opportunity to produce the *Adweek* interview for J.Lo, after which she gave the most beautiful of acceptance speeches for the honor. Sitting behind the camera, listening to Jennifer's speech, I was once again reminded of my conquered fear of being a jack of all trades, master of none.

I realized that in her refusal to be confined to one box, Jennifer had given me permission to show up as my multidimensional, nuanced self. Not just in my career, but in life. Our generation watched Jennifer move from *In Living Color* as a background dancer, to making a cameo in Janet Jackson's music video "That's the Way Love Goes," to her Golden Globe–nominated debut role as Selena, and finally, becoming a globally recognized singer—and Super Bowl halftime performer!—with a catalog full of platinum tracks. Her career has served as one of the most powerfully documented expressions of nuance the industry has ever seen, and one of the greatest examples of thriving in the face of doubters.

During her *Adweek* acceptance speech, one of the most impactful takeaways for me was the following statement: "I've always been more inspired by my goals, even when I was told I can't—which happened more times than I can count." She continued, "As a woman of color who loved to act, to sing, to dance, to create beautiful things, and to touch people's lives, my goal was to never be a brand, but rather to live and stand for something. And while they suggest that you should work to make money in your sleep, my vision is fulfilled by being awake. And to show others that talent combined with hard work and determination will make what they say is impossible, possible."[5]

After producing the spot in Los Angeles, a trip around the block to the Bronx to see Jenny launch her philanthropic venture (Limitless Labs) allowed me to secure an exclusive interview with Ben Affleck. And when I say exclusive interview, I mean we were chopping it up, having a dope conversation while getting to know each other as human beings. In our conversation, he confirmed they were officially a reunited couple and he gave me, and by extension *Adweek*, the exclusive just because he's a good person. Ben Affleck—my personal choice for the best Batman in franchise history—wrote down his personal contact details on a piece of paper and slid it to me across the table to finish our conversation, but this time on the record. The news traveled across the pond and back again, landing on the pages of *Vanity Fair, Vogue, Today, Page Six, People, Marie Claire, Newsweek, E!,* and more, bringing in over 1.4 billion impressions online, and 5.2 million lifetime coverage views.[6]

What's the lesson here? The fact that I was able to secure sponsorship for the music video, hire the crew, refine the budget, and then turn around and attach talent to a publication, craft questions for an interview, and grab an exclusive interview as a journalist reveals the level of nuance inside of me. Why would I ever want to reject or refuse that?

More importantly, why would *you*? If you have various gifts, choose nuance! Stay open to the variety of ways they might be used.

Coming in *hot* at number three on my list of secrets to becoming the star of your own life is *nuance*—a flavorful ingredient within the recipe of becoming the star of your own life! On the following pages, you'll find tips to help develop and champion the nuance within.

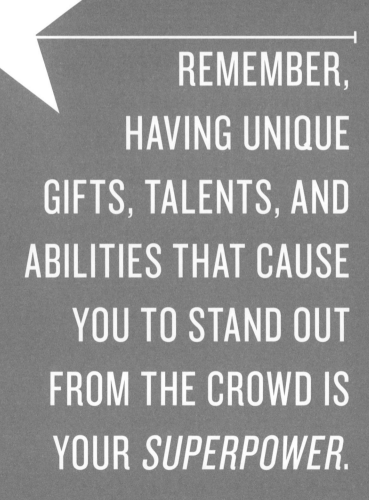

REMEMBER, HAVING UNIQUE GIFTS, TALENTS, AND ABILITIES THAT CAUSE YOU TO STAND OUT FROM THE CROWD IS YOUR *SUPERPOWER*.

FIVE WAYS

TO LEAN INTO *NUANCE*

DIVORCE YOURSELF FROM BINARY THINKING

The world doesn't have to be black or white as binary thinking leads us to believe. We can instead choose to see the world as beautiful shades of gray. In a society that often pressures us to be *one* thing, binary thinking ties us to belief systems or versions of ourselves that may no longer serve us. To divorce yourself from binary thinking, and allow yourself to flourish as a multidimensional human being, spend time journaling about the variety of gifts you possess.

TRY NEW THINGS

As comforting as it may be, especially for those who deal with anxiety, try your best to not get locked into the same routines day in and day out. Step out of your comfort zone and try new things, things that challenge you and bring out different versions of yourself. Today, switch up your routine—to the degree that you're able—to *do it differently.* You may be surprised at what you find!

LEAVE ROOM FOR GROWTH

Just because it's the way it's always been doesn't mean it's the way it always has to be. I encourage you to challenge your way of thinking, questioning the *why* behind what you do. In your journal, spend time looking at your regular routine—hour by hour—and be willing to ask *why* you do what you do. The answers may lead you to growing into the best possible version of yourself.

EMBRACE WHAT MAKES YOU UNIQUE

What are the things that make you unique and quirky? What makes you different than your BFF? These qualities may possibly be the things about yourself that you try to suppress. But those are your superpowers! In your journal, I want you to name, honor, and celebrate the qualities that make you special. Dare to be different.

WELCOME VARIETY

Variety is the spice of life that gives us all flavor. Diversifying our life's palate only enriches our human experience. It would be a shame to leave this earth, never having experienced it in its fullness. Push yourself to diversify your life, your gifts, your talents, your dreams, and your way of being. This week, choose to embrace one thing—starting up a conversation with a stranger, hitting the roller-skating rink, or throwing axes. Anything that feels uncomfortable. The journey of self-discovery is absolutely one worth taking.

QUESTIONS
for Reflection

What are my unique gifts that allow me to stand apart from the crowd?

How can I have a differentiated presence in the marketplace?

How can I better embrace what makes me special?

In which relationships and spaces do I hold myself back? Where do I fail to show up as my fully nuanced self?

What steps can I take to ensure I live a fully nuanced life?

What ways can I be more clear about naming and owning what makes me nuanced?

AFFIRMATION
for Nuance

I AM A MULTIDIMENSIONAL, MULTIFACETED HUMAN being. With grace and ease, I permit myself to equally explore all of my passions without feeling pressured to choose just one. I silence my inner critic, and the negative opinions of those around me, releasing anything blocking me from being fully expressed. I am a multipassionate creator. Today, all of my talents take the world's stage. Nuance is my portion.

Secret # 4:
FAITH

"THE MIND WILL ALWAYS

BOMBARD YOU WITH QUESTIONS

WHEN YOU ATTEMPT TO BELIEVE

IN YOURSELF. BUT IT IS THE LIGHT

OF FAITH THAT ILLUMINATES

THE TRUTH THAT WE SHOULD

KEEP MOVING FORWARD."

—TEAMSOUL

The Grammys are music's biggest night. Leading up to that night, music's biggest stars descend upon the city of Los Angeles to attend the esteemed parties in celebration of their peers and various achievements in the industry. Early on in my LA journey, I was gearing up to attend a Grammy party or two—which was *wild* because I wasn't invited to any of them!

By nature, I'm not a partier. My idea of a good party includes sitting on the couch and watching reruns of my favorite 1990s sitcoms. I did, however, see one event on social media for a pre-Grammy party called Kelly Price & Friends Unplugged: For the Love of R & B. As I read about it, something inside gently urged me to attend—even though I wasn't on the list, nor did I know anyone to get me in. Following that nudge, I got dressed in my Grammys best and headed to the venue. When I arrived, there was a parking spot right out front. And anyone who knows LA parking knows what a miracle that was in itself.

Sitting outside of the event in my parked car, I thought to myself, *You must be crazy to come here with no connections to get in!* I started my engine and got ready to leave, but I once again felt that feeling and surrendered to it. I got out of the car, walked right up to the door, and the doorman asked for my name.

Before I could answer, my good friend, publicist extraordinaire Phyllis Caddell, walked up and said, "Steve, what are you doing here? Come with me!"

She gave me a wristband, and I entered the party—just like that! Minutes later, none other than Whitney Houston walked through that same door. Raising her hand in the air she proclaimed, "Party over here!" I reached up and grabbed her hand, interlocking fingers. Her

PR team then directed her downstairs to the *real* party. Naturally, I followed suit.

Being in the company of one of my favorite musical artists was surreal. A dream come true. She took to the stage for an impromptu performance of her favorite hymn, "Jesus Loves Me." I filmed it on my iPhone and uploaded it to YouTube as she took her seat. The evening began to wind down, and Whitney and her daughter, Bobbi Kristina, began to head for the door. As they pushed past me, I said, "May God bless you both." They in turn embraced me with the warmest hugs, responding, "And may God bless you too," as they exited the building.

No one in the room could know that just thirty-six hours later, Whitney would no longer be with us.

The video I had previously posted of her performing was the only digital account of what became her final performance.[1] As a result, I received a call from CNN to be a guest commentator on *Don Lemon Tonight*, *Anderson Cooper 360°*, and CNN's sister network, HLN, opposite Nancy Grace and AJ Hammer.[2] In a moment when the world turned its back on Whitney, choosing to magnify her struggles instead of acknowledging her vast musical legacy, it was an honor to advocate on her behalf on a global platform. Those appearances on CNN and the subsequent doors that opened up in my career as a result wouldn't have happened had I not stepped out in faith and believed that I would get into the party in the first place.

One of my favorite quotes credited to Dr. Martin Luther King Jr. reads, "Faith is taking the first step even when you don't see the whole staircase."[3] And in my case, faith was showing up at an event I wasn't invited to, believing that a way in would be made.

The fourth secret to becoming the star of your own life is *faith*. When I say "faith," I'm describing a belief in yourself and also a belief in your ability to reach your highest potential to make an impact on this world. Also, faith, for me, is deeply anchored in my belief in a higher power. It's trusting that my steps are ordered and that everything is always happening for my greatest good. Unable to be explained by reason or logic, faith is a feeling, deeply embedded within our DNA, in the very fiber of our beings. Just as vital as oxygen is to the body, without faith, we wouldn't be able to breathe. Faith empowers us to believe that we have an expected end when it seems all is lost. When life gets hard and we face insurmountable challenges, faith is that knowledge that things will indeed get better. Faith is the golden thread that binds us all together inside the fabric of this human experience. What I'm trying to say here is, faith is a pillar within the structural foundation of our human existence, and necessary for our survival. Don't leave home without it.

Are you familiar with the famous French tightrope walker Charles Blondin? Blondin came to fame for his daredevil stunts in the late 1800s. Imagine with me, if you will, that you are at Niagara Falls in 1859, watching Charles walk a tightrope while pushing a wheelbarrow, 190 feet above the falls, spanning 1,100 feet![4] Amazing, right? After he walked safely back and forth numerous times, he asked for a volunteer to sit in a wheelbarrow while he pushed it across the falls. At that moment, the volunteer would probably have had faith in Blondin's abilities, as Blondin had demonstrated them—many times over—already. But faith still had to come into play; the volunteer had to believe, against very high stakes, that Blondin would keep him alive and get him across the falls. Faith had to get him into the wheelbarrow.[5]

My friend, when you have faith in what's possible, you're going to gather your courage—Secret #1—and get in the proverbial wheelbarrow.

For me personally, faith is not a magical concept that I lean into for the sake of appearing spiritually evolved, but rather a prerequisite for my sanity. I've been through too many disappointments, heartbreaks, and betrayals on my path to success to not believe in something greater than myself, guiding me on my journey. It takes extreme faith to overcome disappointment and hardship, choosing to believe that the greatest chapters of your life have yet to be written. But the alternative, living in bitterness, anger, and toxicity, is far worse. My greatest disappointments have come from those I trusted, or called friends, who saw me as nothing more than an opportunity or a means to an end, versus recognizing me as a human being with thoughts, feelings, and emotions. We all have to be careful of those who are attracted to the light on us instead of the light within us.

I'm convinced that when your intentions are pure, and your heart remains open, what is meant for you won't pass you by. It is my sincere belief that every good and perfect thing that God has planned for each of us already exists in his mind and lives within the very ether of the universe. It is simply our job to download his plan for our life, through faith. Our faith is like Wi-Fi: invisible yet having the power to connect us to infinite and limitless possibilities. When we move in faith, we are our most powerful; when we move in fear, we are at our most vulnerable.

When it comes to the many stars I've interviewed on our Hollywood Confidential stage, no other guest's story has better exemplified the principle of faith than that of Angela Bassett in 2018. She may be best known for her Golden Globe Award–winning performance as Queen Mother in *Black Panther: Wakanda Forever*, or her flame-igniting, scene-stealing monologue in the critically acclaimed film *Waiting to Exhale*. But I remember when she first captured my heart in her soul-stirring, Oscar-nominated, Golden Globe–winning portrayal of the Queen of Rock 'n' Roll, Miss Tina Turner, in the film *What's Love Got to Do with It?*

Angela was bit by the acting bug at the tender age of fifteen. Growing up in St. Petersburg, Florida, she immersed herself in the arts and fell in love with the magic and transformative power of storytelling on the theater's stage.[6] She began to audition for every small role she could get to feed her newfound passion, additionally opting to enroll in her high school theater group. But she told me it was a chance encounter with a man at a program called Upward Bound, whose goal is to equip students to prepare for college entrance, that changed the course of her destiny. The man wrote a letter to Angela's mom, insisting that she apply to Harvard, Yale, and UC Berkley due to a special calling he sensed on her life.[7]

After being accepted to Yale, she was afforded the opportunity to further hone her craft and find her voice as an actress, studying under renowned stage director Lloyd Richards, who cast her in Broadway productions of August Wilson's plays *Ma Rainey's Black Bottom* and *Joe Turner's Come and Gone*. After receiving her bachelor of arts in African American studies and her master of fine arts from the Yale School of Drama, she relocated to Los Angeles and was cast in a string of cult classic films, like *Boyz n the Hood*, where she portrayed Reva Styles, mother to Trey, played by Cuba Gooding Jr., and *Malcolm X*, where she played Dr. Betty Shabazz, the wife of Malcolm X, played by Denzel Washington.

But it was her electrifying performance as Tina Turner that launched her to stardom. And here's where faith truly takes the lead in Angela's journey. When I spoke with Angela about the film, she shared that she auditioned for the role but did not immediately receive the part. For over a month, she worked grueling sixteen-hour days in dance rehearsals and went hard at work in the gym to develop her now famously sculpted biceps to become the character—all without a contract or guarantee that the role was hers. It takes an immeasurable amount of faith to show up and pour your heart and soul into an opportunity, without a guarantee of return on your investment. It takes faith! Thankfully, her work paid off immensely, and a star was born.

When Angela took the stage at Hollywood Confidential, she didn't know what to expect. Our event series isn't the typical panel, but rather an existential experience meant to serve the souls of both our attendees and our honorees. Over 1,900 of her adoring fans flooded the auditorium. So when Bassett took the stage, screams erupted so loudly that it sounded like a rock concert. Excitement and emotion flooded her eyes as she expressed her gratitude. "Thank you for coming out tonight! I didn't know it was going to be like this. This is better than morning coffee!"

When I asked Angela what role her faith played in keeping her grounded in the entertainment industry, she responded, "My faith is everything! The role of my faith and God in my life is very important. It's a circuitous journey, full of peaks and valleys. Sometimes you may have a season of *What's Love* followed by a *Stella Got Her Groove Back* season."

She continued, "Then you may get roles that are less challenging, where I'm playing the boss lady and it's only two days of work. You still show up and give it all you have. You still invest everything you have. But there haven't been many roles that took what *What's Love* did. . . . At one point I thought I would have an aneurysm. I cried and wailed for eighteen straight hours. The last day of the shoot was twenty-five hours—the limo and fight scene between me and Ike Turner. But it's my faith that pulled me through."

And her faith paid off. Literally. In 2021, Angela became the highest-paid actress in network television history, earning just south of $500,000 per episode for her role in the critically acclaimed ABC series *9–1–1*.[8]

Having faith in yourself is paramount. You can reach amazing heights when you move with the type of faith that motivates you to consistently put in the work toward your dreams, even without a guaranteed return on investment. As the saying goes, no risk, no reward! If you know you've been called to it, commit. As a matter of fact, I challenge you to do one thing each day that helps you get closer to your dreams. Go network at that party. Get into the gym. Or start that business. Whatever it is for you, place all of your hopes in the wheelbarrow of faith and trust that they will be made manifest. When you have faith—in what is outside of you and what is inside of you—the possibilities will be endless. So where can your faith lead you?

Securing the number four spot on my list of secrets is *faith*, the chief cornerstone within building the life of your dreams as the star of your own life.

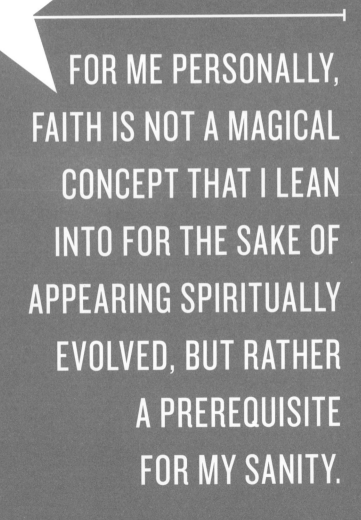

FOR ME PERSONALLY, FAITH IS NOT A MAGICAL CONCEPT THAT I LEAN INTO FOR THE SAKE OF APPEARING SPIRITUALLY EVOLVED, BUT RATHER A PREREQUISITE FOR MY SANITY.

FIVE WAYS

TO BUILD YOUR *FAITH*

ELIMINATE THE NEGATIVE

One of the most powerful tools we have is our words. They have the ability to hurt or to heal. Their meaning shapes our world and creates our reality. Eliminating negative words and phrases from our vocabulary can aid us in pushing past our limited beliefs and help us to stand firm in our faith. Listen up this week for words that escape your lips that may need to go. Jot them down and commit to speaking only what is positive.

LOOK FOR MIRACLES

As you pursue your dreams and goals, raise your level of expectation when it comes to seeing the miraculous in your life. Spend a bit of time recalling those divine appointments, relationships, and experiences that have either opened doors or affirmed your faith and belief in yourself. Write them down and keep your eyes open for what's next.

ABOLISH FEAR

Fear can be a crippling emotion that stifles our journey of faith. When we remove fear from our lives, we make space for faith to reside. Choosing faith over fear does not eradicate that which worries us, but rather offers a solution for how to address and overcome it. As you notice fear creeping in this week, jot it down. Then, above it write, *and speak aloud*, the mantra at the end of this chapter.

PUT ON YOUR BLINDERS OF FAITH

Seeing life through the lens of faith helps us look past our present circumstances and place our trust in the fact that there is a beautiful light at the end of the tunnel. One of my favorite quotes, from Blaise Pascal in *Pensées*, that grounds me is, "In faith, there is enough light for those who want to believe and enough shadows to blind those who don't." This week, set your sights on the light at the end of the tunnel. Share with a friend about what you see there!

PRAYER AND MEDITATION

In prayer, we talk to God. In meditation, we listen. Meditation helps increase our knowledge of divine principles, preserves our faith, and brings us back into remembrance of what we know to be true. Prayer and meditation are wonderful tools to help grow our faith in God, our dreams, and our selves. This week, make an appointment on your calendar to experiment with both.

QUESTIONS
for Reflection

How has fear shown up in my life as a hindrance to reaching my goals?

What are the specific ways in which I can actively choose faith over fear?

When was the last time I listened to my inner voice? When was the last time I shoved down my intuition?

What would my life look like if I welcomed the concept of faith?

What are faith practices that resonate with me that I can lean on when I'm in a hard season?

How can faith better help me download God's divine plan for my life?

AFFIRMATION
for Faith

FAITH IS MY NATURAL STATE OF MIND AND THE ORIGIN of my success. I have faith in myself, and in my ability to make decisions for my life without seeking validation from others. There is no room for fear in my life, as my faith lifts me high above all limiting beliefs, allowing me to achieve the impossible and remain calm in the face of great adversity. As I close the door on the past, I place my faith in the future, believing that everything is always working together for my greatest good.

Secret # 5:
INGENUITY

"INGENUITY, PLUS COURAGE,

PLUS WORK, EQUALS MIRACLES."

—BOB RICHARDS

B y now you know I love a good affirmation, but even more so, a thought-provoking quote! Anyone who follows me on social media knows that I swear by them. But most people don't know my why. The great Dr. Maya Angelou told us that words are things, and they hold a tremendous amount of power. The power to build you up and the power to tear you down. Early on in my career, I was chasing success, not realizing that I had the ability to generate it all on my own. That is until one day, scrolling on social media, I ran into a quote by Howard Schultz that stopped me in my tracks and changed my way of being. It read, "You have the power to change the course of your life, simply by creating what you want to be part of!" The seed of ingenuity was planted within me at that very moment. Almost immediately upon reading those words, I understood the power of building my own platform. And that in doing so, I would never have to worry about being invited to have a seat at anyone else's table, because I could build my own. At that time, I was hosting a then-unknown future Oscar winner on my couch, who had fallen down on their luck in the industry and was desperately in need of a place to stay.

And that wasn't the only person. There had been about two dozen others prior, whom I committed to supporting through industry introductions and financial support, and through the sharing of my resources. Sometimes to depletion. I blame my grandmother, Loda M. Spencer. She was a giver. She would give and give until she was down to her last. And she did so cheerfully. She passed that down to my mom, and my mom passed it down to me. I got it honest. But if there is one thing I've learned the hard way, it's that **givers have to set limits, because takers never will.**

However, it was in those early days of housing and helping so many aspiring actors and creatives that I came to grips with the fact that **if something is bothering me to this degree, I'm more than likely called to be a part of the solution.** But it was going to take some innovative thinking to find a sustainable way to service this community without emptying my bank account and depleting my personal resources. Shortly after, I had a lightbulb moment. The social media quote resurfaced from the recesses of my mind. A vision came to me of building a forum and standing in the gap between aspiring hopefuls and established voices who I hoped would help me on my mission to equip and empower the next generation of leaders. That's when I conceived Hollywood Confidential.

Each of our events reaches over two thousand multicultural "zillennial" attendees, who are afforded the opportunity to network with other brilliant young minds, while receiving hands-on advice and tangible next steps from legends and Hollywood trailblazers they admire.

On these incredibly amazing nights, it's all about our attendees—the next wave of directors, producers, writers, singers, authors, choreographers, and change agents. They may not have achieved enough in the eyes of the industry to attend a Hollywood premiere, but at Hollywood Confidential, we roll out the red carpet just for them—customized activations, gift bags, the ability to be photographed on our step & repeat, access to resources, and practical advice and information that can help change the trajectory of their careers.

We've been fortunate to have had so many future household names pass through our doors pre-fame, stopping by to receive invaluable advice on their respective journeys. When I think of all we have accomplished in just a decade, I am truly overwhelmed and filled with gratitude. I attribute that lightbulb moment to create the series to a moment of divine inspiration. I also name it an act of ingenuity, which is the fifth secret to finally taking ownership of your own life. Ingenuity has been defined as "the quality of being clever, original, and inventive, often involving the process of applying ideas to solve problems or meet challenges."[1] It's the driving force behind solution-oriented thinking that has helped humanity evolve for centuries.

One of the brightest examples of ingenuity in motion that I've come across in my industry is a woman who prides herself on creating fresh solutions to existing problems: the extraordinary Issa Rae. She's the unofficial leader of the new school of self-made creatives, who found massive success by taking her creative genius and intellectual property straight to consumers. She found a way to bypass traditional and archaic systems that have far too often lacked innovation and diversity in their strategy—as well as in their boardrooms.

Issa is the creator of HBO's Emmy-winning, Golden Globe–nominated show *Insecure*, as well as the star of box office hits *Barbie, The Lovebirds, The Hate U Give*, and Oscar-winner *American Fiction*. She's undoubtedly cemented her place in Hollywood history, but her path into the industry has been anything but conventional.

I first met and worked with Issa in 2014, amid the growing popularity of her digital series, *Awkward Black Girl (ABG)*. A self-proclaimed uncomfortable soul, Issa's willingness to unapologetically be herself helped her connect with a severely underserved market of Black women who never felt like they fit into the molds of the twenty-first-century woman as portrayed in mainstream media. Instead, Issa and *ABG* gave women permission to simply *be*, once again proving that the Black experience is indeed *not* monolithic. Launched exclusively on YouTube, written, produced, and funded by Rae through crowdfunding, *ABG's* relatable storylines and comedic stylings began to catch on like wildfire. Its independent success served as a source of inspiration for creatives and signaled a shift within the industry, proving that we can greenlight our *own* concepts and build our *own* audiences without studio and network assistance. We can achieve success on our own terms. How's that for ingenuity?

The irony of Rae's success is that many studios and networks didn't see her vision. Issa received a succession of resounding nos on her show ideas from the powers that be before *ABG* was ever a thought. Several executives gave Issa feedback on her concepts, stating that because the stories were rooted in the Black experience, they weren't relatable and that there was no audience for her content. Marginalized voices, communities, and stories are often considered irrelevant, unmarketable, and off-brand—until they aren't. See the successes of *Black Panther, Get Out, Girls Trip, Moonlight,* and more. Faced with the choice between watering down her ideas to fit within a mainstream template to secure a deal, or independently moving forward with the vision of normalizing Black stories, she chose the latter, and the rest is history.

Just like Issa, we have all been presented with the option of fitting within a particular mold thought best for us by others, *or* taking the risk of betting on ourselves to blaze our own path where a trail may not exist. The opinions of family, friends, society, and external pressures often weigh on the decisions we make, the path we choose, and how we show up in the world. It takes bravery, discipline, belief in oneself, and a whole lot of audacity to shatter the mold of traditionalism and venture down the road less traveled.

I lovingly nicknamed Issa the "Harriet Tubman of TV and film," as she specializes in charting new paths to freedom through storytelling and has made it a point to bring like-minded individuals alongside her on the journey. Like myself, she prides herself on serving and holding space for creatives of color in the industry to help them achieve their dreams. By identifying new and emerging voices via her management company, Color Creative, and producing stories from marginalized communities through her entertainment company, Hoorae Media, Issa has become a true disrupter and force within the industry.[2]

I consider myself to be a well-adjusted, spiritually evolved person (depending on the day and circumstance). Through my process of spiritual maturation, I've acquired a belief that we are closest to and most like God when we create. In this lifetime, we have a very unique opportunity to become co-creators with God, by birthing and implementing new ideas. Taking an idea from inside your head and bringing it into reality is not only a spiritual experience but a massive accomplishment!

Ten years ago, when I created Hollywood Confidential, I had no idea that the event would become what it is today. The event series is free of charge for attendees, because I can't say that I feel called to help young dreamers and then tax their aspirations. Especially when most of them are trying to figure out how to pay their rent and afford acting classes, headshots, and three meals a day. What that means is that in addition to having the ingenuity to conceive the event, I've also needed to practice ingenuity in funding the event. Drawing on my marketing background, I decided to pursue corporate sponsorships with brands like Walgreens, Dove, L'Oréal, and a host of other globally recognized corporations early on in my career. And so Hollywood Confidential remains free to those who attend. We put the flyer out to the general public via social media, attendees are able to RSVP at no charge, and seven days later, we host the event!

I'll be the first to admit that Hollywood Confidential does not have the patent on panels. They began way before I was born and will be here long after I'm gone. But what makes our series so special is that we bring together a room full of dreamers and provide them with the tools to harness their dreams and bring their dreams into reality. We've been able to create a pipeline for the next generation of storytellers to be championed. And we're giving young dreamers the opportunity to directly interface with legendary talent who have a heart to see their potential actualized.

When I interviewed Issa at Hollywood Confidential, at the legendary Saban Theater in Beverly Hills, she had just completed the first season of *Insecure*, which she both created and starred in. The anticipation was high, as many wanted to hear her journey of creating her own path to mainstream success. Over 2,100 African American, Asian, Caucasian, and Latinx attendees filled the room with sheer anticipation. And Issa did not disappoint. When I asked her about creating her own opportunities, and the magic of leaning into her gift of ingenuity for optimal achievement, she responded, "My individuality is a currency . . . and that's what people are investing in."[3] *Boom!*

Issa is a true trailblazer who is steadily building a growing empire on her own terms.

When the industry told her *no,* she created her very own *yes.* I'm moved by her relentless pursuit of her dreams. The resiliency and ingenuity displayed throughout each chapter of her story helped her move past disappointment into fulfillment. With a handful of connections and limited resources, Issa attracted the right opportunities into her life *by being her most genuine self.* That innovativeness resonated with a niche market, who became her core audience of supporters, and subsequently brought her worldwide acclaim. Thank you, Issa, for being a wonderful reminder of the power of ingenuity, and a tangible example of all of the wonderful possibilities that live just on the other side of rejection.

We must never underestimate our ability to make our own way, solve problems, and find creative ways to serve others. Ingenuity helps us tap into that reservoir of creativity within us. Where curiosity is encouraged, ingenuity resides, and solutions thrive.

If you want to thrive, lay hold of number five on my list of secrets to becoming the star of your own life. We can truly build the life of our dreams by allowing creativity and ingenuity to serve as a conduit to fulfillment.

On the next page you'll find five tips from me on how to lead with ingenuity!

WHERE CURIOSITY
IS ENCOURAGED,
INGENUITY RESIDES,
AND SOLUTIONS
THRIVE.

FIVE WAYS

TO PRACTICE *INGENUITY*

BE RESILIENT

Ingenuity and failure are the best of friends. You can't have one without the other. Get comfortable with taking shots that may not land, for it's in our practice that we are made perfect. Make a list of the failures you've experienced and decide how you'll begin to use ingenuity to your advantage!

EMBRACE NEW IDEAS

Old ways won't open new doors. Be receptive to embracing new ways, cracking new codes, and applying fresh perspectives! In whatever work you are doing *today*—whether it's waiting tables, serving as an assistant on set, or chasing a toddler—find ways that you might begin to do it in a fresh way.

PUSH BOUNDARIES

Don't be afraid to think outside the box! When we push past the limits of possibility, we can achieve the impossible. One exercise to help you think beyond the box is to brainstorm one hundred new ways to do a thing!

PRACTICE PERSISTENCE

No matter the profession, the universal thread found within successful individuals around the world is that of persistence. Remaining steadfast in pursuit of your goals can truly lead to a major reward. Endure! Has there been a dream that you've let go of? What forgotten dream might you need to pick up today?

STAY CURIOUS

Curiosity is one of the most powerful tools we have in our arsenal of creativity! The hallmarks of innovative thinking, curiosity, and ingenuity work in tandem to help us reach new heights and achieve new goals in an ever-changing, fast-paced world. Because I suspect there's been at least one question you've had about the dream you want to pursue, do a deep dive today to get the answer.

QUESTIONS
for Reflection

What resources do I already have in my hands, right now, as I read this book that can help me reach my goals?

How can I be more of my unapologetic self, to help align and attract the right opportunities and situations?

What risks can I take to increase my opportunities for growth?

How can I build relationships with people who have already achieved what I aspire to do?

What goals can I set up each day that will help me consistently show up in the world as my best self?

AFFIRMATION
for Ingenuity

AN ENDLESS RESERVOIR OF CREATIVITY LIES WITHIN me, flowing throughout every aspect of my life. I am a co-creator with God, and together, we can effortlessly create the opportunities I wish to receive. When I am vulnerable, allowing my thoughts to come from the loving space inside my heart, I am consciously directing my creative compass to bring about life-changing opportunities. Ingenious ideas and solutions easily come to me daily. There is no challenge or obstacle on the path before me that I cannot overcome. Creativity is a conduit to fulfillment and the bridge to the life of my dreams.

Secret # 6 :

DETACHMENT

"THE TRUE MEANING OF OPENING
OUR HEART IS THAT WE NO LONGER
HAVE FEAR OF LOSING ANYTHING.
IT IS A FORM OF SURRENDER . . .
[OF] OUR HOPES AND FEARS, AND
AN INVESTMENT IN OUR MISERY.
WHEN WE HAVE REACHED THE
FINAL POINT OF THAT SURRENDER
THERE IS NOTHING THAT WE
WANT TO HOLD ON TO."

—ANAM THUBTEN

Would you believe me if I told you that the best way to get something is to not want it at all? No really, it's true! Think about it. Many of our problems are in direct connection with our need to attach ourselves to that which is fleeting. Sometimes we can want something so badly that we sabotage it. Our overzealousness can smother the life out of the most voracious of dreams, and our unhealthy attachments can become the very chains that bind us. This is the embodiment of the Buddha quote, "The root of suffering is attachment."

The sixth secret to becoming the star of your own life is *detachment*! The Law of Detachment—also referred to as the Principle of Freedom[1]—states that in order to manifest our desires, we must release attachment to the outcome itself as well as to the path we might take to get there.[2] Simply put, once we lean into embracing life's unknown variables, we become a clear vessel and channel for manifestation. Detachment is also about surrendering to the *flow* of life and relinquishing the need for control. The process of surrender includes trusting that everything that happens in your life is working for your highest good at all times.

We can want something so bad that we can get in our own way. And yet when we release our expectations, when we release how we think it has to happen, we make space for the miraculous. When we're able to detach from the outcome, when we can surrender it, we prepare ourselves to receive what's truly ours. We open ourselves to experience the magic. If you're open to experimenting with this secret, you can say to yourself, aloud, "I know that what God has for me is for me, but this might not be the path, and I'm open to whatever's next."

My favorite example of surrender comes from Oprah Winfrey. It would be impossible to capture the richness of her full story here, so let's look at a highlight reel. Born in the rural town of Kosciusko, Mississippi, she was named after the biblical figure Orpah, which quickly became "Oprah," as it was easier to pronounce. Growing up in a small Wisconsin community with her mother, she had a troubled adolescence, as she was sexually abused by a number of male relatives. Winfrey ultimately relocated to Nashville as a teen, to live with her father, Vernon, a barber and businessman, who offered her a deeper sense of stability and safety.

After high school, Winfrey enrolled in Tennessee State University to obtain her bachelor's degree in speech communications and performing arts. While in school, she began working in radio and television broadcasting, developing a deep passion for the craft. She eventually relocated to a bigger market, Baltimore, Maryland, to host the talk show *People Are Talking.* The show became a huge hit for eight long seasons. So much so that she was recruited by a Chicago TV station to host the morning show *AM Chicago,* which famously became *The Oprah Winfrey Show.*

But before the massive success of the show, Oprah said she got a copy of Alice Walker's book *The Color Purple.* To her surprise, the lead character's story struck a chord with her own hardships, which gave her an intrinsic connection to the novel. She purchased several copies and passed them out to strangers.

After hearing that Quincy Jones and Steven Spielberg were set to adapt the book into a movie, Winfrey vowed to be part of the project by any means necessary, even though she had no professional acting experience whatsoever. As fate would have it, Jones saw her on *AM Chicago* and sent tapes to Steven Spielberg, and she was cast in the role of Sofia.[3] After reading

WHEN WE'RE ABLE TO
DETACH FROM THE
OUTCOME, WHEN WE CAN
SURRENDER IT, WE PREPARE
OURSELVES TO RECEIVE
WHAT'S TRULY OURS.

for the part, two full months went by and she hadn't heard any feedback. She phoned the casting director, only to be told that *real* actresses were auditioning for the role—specifically, the very talented Alfree Woodard.

Deducing that she would not get the part, Oprah enrolled herself in a fat farm, assuming that the reason she was passed over for the movie was due to her weight. As she was running around the track at the farm, she began to have a conversation with God. Feeling betrayed, as she felt like all the signs had been pointing to the fact that the role was hers, she realized she had to surrender her greatest desire. Yes, she had desperately wanted the role, but she'd come to a point where she was willing to release it. She began to sing the hymn "I Surrender All." With tears streaming down her face, she accepted what was and let go of what could have been. And it was at *that moment* that someone came running out to her on the track to tell her that the casting director was on the phone for her, to offer her the role of Sofia. The casting director also told her that if she lost one pound, she could lose the role. On her way home from the fat farm, she stopped at Dairy Queen, just in case it was real![4]

That, my friends, is detachment in motion.

The success of the film bolstered her fame and likely helped *The Oprah Winfrey Show* to succeed, placing her on the path to becoming the biggest media mogul in the world. Her ability to detach from her biggest dream actually helped shift her life.

Have you ever wanted something *so badly* that you can taste it? For years, I knew I was called to the space of entertainment. I'm not kidding when

I say that I was born for this. No lie. I can remember when I was twelve years old, I would arrange for my sister and my female cousins to learn the lyrics and latest dance moves to the biggest songs of the day and put on a performance for the boys in the neighborhood. Charging twenty-five cents per viewer, I would call myself the girls' "manager," profiting just enough to buy each of us a pack of Now and Later candy and a cold Clearly Canadian soda pop from the corner store. In my adult life, I then went on to work with some of the biggest girl groups the world has ever known. If you are a parent, and you want to assist in guiding your child into purpose, all you have to do is watch what they naturally gravitate toward to inform you of who they are destined to be. The soul always knows, and deep down within my soul, at a very young age, was the heart of an entrepreneur.

When I relocated to Los Angeles, I was established, and business was thriving. But when I decided to transition out of marketing and into full-time production, I hit a brick wall. I emptied out my savings and was down to my last dollar.

Admitting defeat, I made peace with the fact that I had done all I could do and had made some great memories by taking a risk on myself. I was proud. I looked up flights to head back to Ohio and decided to attend one last event before leaving the city. The event, thrown by Robi Reed, the sole African American Emmy Award–winning casting director, was titled Sunshine Beyond Summer, and was an annual benefit for various health and wellness initiatives. Atypically for me, I was throwing drinks *back* at the bar, drowning my sorrows, when Grammy-winning jazz and R & B artist Ledisi called everyone to the dance floor. While performing her hit single "Alright," she pointed to me and called out my name, sharing that she felt led to encourage me and that everything was indeed going to be all right. I chuckled to myself thinking, *Of course it will be. The struggle is over. I'm going home!*

After the performance, I found myself sitting next to Hollywood royalty—the Oscar-nominated director John Singleton, creator of some of my all-time favorite movies like *Boyz n the Hood, Poetic Justice,* and *Baby Boy.* Sitting next to him was Kimberly Elise, a critically acclaimed actress who starred in another one of my top-five favorite movies, *Set It Off,* opposite Queen Latifah. Before I knew it, we had hit it off, and I found myself pitching my services. I walked away from the event with a brand-new retainer client in Kimberly Elise, which extended my Los Angeles shelf life. Ledisi was right!

That account got me through the door at VH1, where I helped launch their first scripted show, *Hit the Floor,* starring Kimberly Elise, and their first scripted biopic, *CrazySexyCool: The TLC Story,* featuring Keke Palmer as Chilli. VH1 also ended up becoming my very first media sponsor for Hollywood Confidential, where Kimberly and Keke were my very first panelists. The rest, as they say, is history. In that moment when I was detaching from Los Angeles and the career I imagined for myself there, I was given the opportunity to move forward.

All my life, I've loved Oprah Winfrey. And for years, I visualized myself as a guest on the couch of *The Oprah Winfrey Show*—the quintessential goal of millennials who had a dream of being successful. Oprah was going to discover *me*! Since she was one of the most successful female talk show hosts of color in the history of daytime television, a lot of us placed our hopes and dreams on her shoulders, which must have been an unbearable weight to carry.

When *The Oprah Winfrey Show* came to an end in 2011, and I hadn't "made it" yet? Man, talk about upset! Who was going to interview me now? *And does this mean I won't be getting a car?* I shuddered to think. Alongside the dreams of millions officially deferred, I continued to pursue my goals and work hard. What I didn't know then was that years later I would produce three shows on her network, prompting OWN to extend an invitation for me to attend the taping of *Oprah Winfrey Presents: When They See Us.* Not only did I attend, but I sat in the front row, lending me the opportunity to interact directly with Oprah, and I was even asked a question from the stage. Just another fun example of where my long-ago detachment eventually led me! Things might not happen when we want them to, but they always happen within the divine timing of life.

Wherever you are on the journey to becoming the star of your life, today I encourage you to assume a posture of detachment. It doesn't mean you don't care. It doesn't mean you don't hustle. It doesn't mean you don't do the work. What it does mean is that when you're willing to say, "I'm open to whatever's next," you are opening yourself to receive what is truly for you.

Debuting at number six on my list, this has been a lesson on how you can use the principle of detachment to play a major role in helping you become the star of your own life.

FOUR WAYS

TO PRACTICE *DETACHMENT*

PRACTICE LETTING GO

You've heard the saying, "If you love something, let it go." Truer words have never been spoken. It's in letting go of expectations and outcomes that we find true emotional freedom, no longer controlled by our mountaintop highs or valley lows. We instead focus on the journey as a whole, accepting what comes as we move forward on our destined paths. Write a bit in your journal about what you might need to let go of today.

EMBRACE THE UNKNOWN

By leaning into the power of life's unknown variables, we can find true security. When we surrender our need for control, we welcome divine guidance as our compass, directing our path to the desires of our heart. (Tonight, in the mirror, speak aloud the Affirmation for Detachment at the end of this chapter.)

ACCEPT WHAT IS

It's been said that acceptance is having the faith, despite all circumstances, that all is well. When we accept what is, without trying to manipulate a particular outcome, we leave space for God to work his divine plan in our lives. What is it, today, that you need to choose to *accept*, as it is?

BE PATIENT WITH YOUR UNLEARNING

If you find yourself outside of the flow of life, and trying to force a particular outcome, be gentle with yourself. Rome wasn't built in a day, and neither will your process of unlearning. It's through the constant examination and observation of our thoughts that we become mindful, allowing us to let go of attachments and cultivate an inner peace that won't be impacted by external circumstances. When you catch those thoughts to be unlearned, jot them down in your journal.

QUESTIONS
for Reflection

What attachments are in my life that may be leading to my own suffering?

How can I better operate in *flow* (not the force) of life?

What areas of my life am I controlling that I can surrender to God?

What affirmations can I recite to remind myself that, no matter how far I feel from my goals, I'm exactly where I need to be?

AFFIRMATION
for Detachment

I AM CONNECTED TO EVERYTHING AND ATTACHED TO nothing. I relinquish the need for control in my life and surrender to this present moment. When I lean into the magic and mystery of the unknown, I consciously create space and opportunity to manifest the life of my dreams.

Secret #1:
ENDURANCE

"ENDURANCE IS ONE OF THE MOST
DIFFICULT DISCIPLINES, BUT IT IS
TO THE ONE WHO ENDURES THAT
THE FINAL VICTORY COMES."

—UNKNOWN

W hat do you know about long-distance running? Just as mental as it is physical, endurance running is a complete and total workout of the body and the mind, designed to test the limits of runners over the course of long and grueling hours and miles. Running causes wear and tear on multiple joints at the same time, often leading to body fatigue. Without the proper rest, nutrition, and preparation, you've set yourself up for failure. And sometimes it's not your body that gives out, it's your mind. Mental fatigue is real. Without the proper mindset, it's impossible to finish a long-distance run. Although challenging, long-distance running comes with great rewards, including increased confidence, mental fortitude, and a myriad of health benefits.

Once we begin to look at our lives, and the pursuit of our dreams and goals, through the framing of a long-distance marathon, we gain invaluable perspective and strategy to help us win our race. With a steady pace, the right perspective, a healthy mindset, and an unwavering sense of determination, we can and will succeed. When we embrace the journey toward becoming the stars of our own lives as the *marathon* of our lives, rather than the sprint, our desire for instant gratification subsides, and we begin to set in motion a series of long-term sustainable and inevitable victories.

Recently I was introduced to the ancient concept of *gaman*, a Japanese principle or way of thinking that urges one to power through difficult circumstances without complaint or objection—understanding that true strength lies inside our ability to navigate tough times with grace and honor. In essence, the principle mandates that we keep a positive outlook, while practicing patience and endurance, even when things seem hopeless. And man, has this helped me shift my perspective on the marathon of a career journey I've been on! It's been said that it takes over ten years to become an overnight success, but what happens when it takes several decades to reach your peak? Will you stay committed, or will you forfeit the prize and all you've worked toward before reaching the finish line? That's a question I've had to grapple with a time or two on my long and winding road to success. And perhaps you have too. What I know to be true is that **each time we reach toward our goals, even if we don't succeed, we make a spiritual deposit into our bank of opportunities.** Eventually, we'll be able to make a withdrawal that cannot be denied.

One actress whose career has gone the distance in Hollywood is the talented Regina King. A scepter in her left hand, director's slate in her right, the world has become subject to her reign and majesty. With one look at her impressive resume and outstanding accomplishments, it's abundantly clear that she was born to rule and dominate the stage and screen.

With over fifty film and TV credits, including *Jerry Maguire, Legally Blonde 2, Watchmen,* and *If Beale Street Could Talk,* it's clear Regina has the Midas touch. The Oscars and Emmys have crowned her work supreme. And her recent expansion into the field of directing has proven to be a historic trek, marking the second time an African American woman has been nominated for a Golden Globe for Best Director.[1]

In the business since she was a teen, Regina was in her forties when she began to receive the critical acclaim and recognition that she deserves. What that means is that she showed up *and* did the work, year after year.

And then, one day, things shifted. I don't know that a lot of us are willing to *endure* in that way, to put in that much time before we make it.

I do want to say that we, as a community, have always seen, celebrated, and championed her gift, so now that the mainstream has caught up and joined arms in our sheer adoration of this icon, it truly feels like a win for us all. Something has to be said for graciously waiting your turn. I can imagine that there were times when she became frustrated with the long and tedious process. But when you're in tune with your gift and purpose, and you understand that endurance is the name of the game— there is a knowing that success is imminent. Maybe not immediately, but definitely. When we endure, we always win.

Regina, whose name even means "queen," never allowed her crown to slip as she waited her turn at overseeing the kingdom. She understood the power in consistency, as well as the concept of seed time and harvest. When we plant seeds, we can't determine the time at which they'll sprout, but we do know that if we continue to plant seeds there *will* be a harvest. Every role, great or small, led to the next opportunity, increasing her skillset and setting the stage for the next iteration of her success story. Now in her prime, Regina continues to kick down doors for herself, and for women of color who aspire to follow in her footsteps. She has left an indelible mark on this industry as one of the greatest storytellers of the twenty-first century—and the best part is, she's just getting started.

I first fell in love with Regina when she was on *227*, starring as Brenda Jenkins, the sassy and outspoken teenage daughter of comedic legend Marla Gibbs—who was our esteemed honoree at our Hollywood Confidential ten-year anniversary. After *227* was cancelled, work stalled for King. In our interview, she explained, "At that time in my career so many people in the business thought I was Brenda of *227*; in real life, I was severely type-cast and it didn't give me the opportunity to show what I could do or express the gift God had given me." When she was offered the opportunity to audition for *Boyz n the Hood*, after three lines the casting director said, "Oh, I just wanted to see if you could be street." Regina explained, "Girl, if all I had to do was be hood, I could have gave you that at the door!"[2]

My love affair with Regina *really* grew when, a few years after *Boyz n the Hood*, she starred in *Poetic Justice* opposite Janet Jackson as Iesha, the round-the-way girl with that undeniable south central LA swagger. Something about those braids and gold hoop earrings did it for me.

Long before we collaborated on Hollywood Confidential, I was stoked to meet Regina by complete happenstance back in 2010 at an open mic event hosted by our mutual friend, actress Tichina Arnold. I struck up a conversation, which later led to working together professionally. Of all the celebrities I've met, Regina has this down-to-earth quality that makes her feel like a lovable friend, aunty, sister, or homegirl you grew up with from the neighborhood. She is just solid people.

Regina's career ascension is the culmination of endurance. With each audition, with each role, and with every rejection she faced, she was making a spiritual investment into the life of her dreams, which has now been made manifest on the world's stage. Simply put, my girl is ca$hing out! Her determination has carried her through many seasons, and I believe, for her, and for us all, the very best season is yet to come.

In 2017, on the heels of a pair of Emmy wins, Regina humbly accepted the invitation to grace our stage at Hollywood Confidential, where I had a chance to speak candidly with her about how the process of waiting stretched her, not only as an artist but also as a human being. As she shared, "Throughout my journey, I've learned so much about myself and what I'm capable of. And that's important—to expand, to evolve, and to push yourself to the limits. Comfort zones are where dreams go to die. If you remain in a safe or comfortable place, you're never going to grow. And life is so much more fun when you are growing. I wouldn't change a thing." She really brought it home for our audience of aspiring talents when she said, "There is no secret to success. You can line up thirty successful people, and every story on how they got there is different. But the common denominator between each story is that they remained committed."[3] (For someone who doesn't believe there's a secret to success, I think she just dropped Secret #7!)

Your journey is different from Regina's and it's different from mine. So what does endurance look like for you? May I suggest that, like long-distance runners, you'll need to adequately prepare for the tedious journey ahead. Preparation means that you keep doing the work. You keep showing up. And because that process does require energy, you practice self-care along the way, which might mean taking a pit stop to refuel. But whatever you do, don't quit, as chances are your breakthrough will be found on the other side of enduring. Finish strong!

Hanging in there at the number seven spot of my list of secrets to becoming the star of your own life is *endurance*.

FIVE WAYS

TO PRACTICE *ENDURANCE*

CHART YOUR SUCCESS PLAN

When we fail to plan, we plan to fail. Having a strategy is key to reaching your goals. And having a strategic plan in place helps you to pace yourself as you endure, powering through this journey called life. List the areas of your life in which you can begin to strategize today.

CELEBRATE MILESTONES

Celebrate your wins, even the small ones! Celebrations serve as markers of progress, which help to break down milestones into manageable goals. Whether you've had an article accepted for publication or scored a role in a community theater production, celebrate a little win today by toasting glasses with a friend.

STAY HYDRATED

Finding ways to remain passionate about your goals will help to ensure you don't quit before the mission is complete. Remembering why you started and what brought you to this point can serve as the extra push you need to get you over the finish line. To stay hydrated for the rest of the race, write down why you set off at the starting line in the first place.

REFUEL

When running your race, don't be scared to take a pause and recharge yourself. Exhaustion and fatigue are a real thing. Don't burn yourself out for the sake of completing a task. What good is achievement if we aren't spiritually, mentally, and physically sound to enjoy it? Today, build a rest—whether it's three hours, or three days—into your schedule.

FIND A RUNNING MATE

The African proverb from Burkina Faso says, "If you want to go fast, go alone. But if you want to go far, go together." Building community with like-minded people who have similar goals can be essential in completing your charted course. Don't underestimate the power of a true friend to help you endure the many challenges of life. This week, contact one person who's running a race similar to yours, and meet up to strategize next steps.

QUESTIONS
for Reflection

How can I better pace myself to ensure I endure until the end?

What are practical ways that I can stay passionate about my goals?

What are ways I can refuel and practice self-care when I feel burnt out on my path?

What are a few practical ways that I can celebrate my accomplishments and milestones, big or small?

Who are my running mates that can help me go further and push across the finish line?

AFFIRMATION
for Endurance

AS I RUN MY RACE, I DO SO WITH THE UNDERSTAND-
ing that my reward is equally found in how I handle
the journey as it is in reaching the destination. Having
endurance and discipline in life shortens the distance
to reaching my goals. And with hard work, determination, and a healthy mindset, winning is inevitable. I
will remain steadfast and unmovable in the pursuit of
my dreams, knowing that good things truly do come to
those who are consistent.

Secret # 8 :
NEGATIVITY

"THERE IS TRANSFORMATIVE POWER
IN DARKNESS. EVEN IN THE ABSENCE
OF LIGHT, THERE LIES OPPORTUNITY
FOR GROWTH, SELF-DISCOVERY, AND
ULTIMATELY, FINDING OUR WAY TO
THE BRILLIANCE THAT AWAITS US."

—UNKNOWN

o, you may be thinking, *How is negativity a secret I need to embrace to become the star of my own life, Steve?* To that I say, "You face your greatest opposition when you're the closest to your biggest miracle." Those words, tweeted by Bishop T. D. Jakes,[1] speak to the seemingly insurmountable number of challenges, difficulties, and dark moments we will face in pursuit of our dreams. But I'm comforted by the fact that, without darkness, we'd never see the stars shining brightly in the night sky. Let's get into the surprising yet necessary power of negativity on our journeys and see what's on the other side.

I believe that all the world is a stage, and at a divinely appointed time, we meet and join forces with a great ensemble cast, who both enter and exit our lives to assist us in playing our parts to the best of our ability. But above all, I wholeheartedly believe that, within that ensemble cast, villains play a significant role in the growth of our souls.

No matter your spiritual beliefs, you likely know the story of Jesus and his closest friends, the twelve disciples. Jesus prepared his entire life to use his gifts and talents on earth, and in his thirty-third year, it was finally time to fulfill his purpose. As the story goes, one of his closest friends, Judas, betrayed him, selling him out for just thirty pieces of silver and disclosing his location to government authorities. After Jesus was apprehended, he was put on the cross and sacrificed. But it was through his death that he was able to ascend to his next and greatest act—Savior of the world. You see, my friends, the great opposition, the betrayal, was *key* in his ascension.

Senior Kabbalah teacher David Ghiyam said, "There is a spiritual law in Kabbalah that when someone speaks badly about you, true or not, and you accept it, don't react, and embrace the pain, the other person takes away some of the negativity that was part of your soul."[2] Counterintuitive, right? You don't react, but you instead embrace the pain. Through this process, the other person takes away—or *receives*—some of the negativity that was part of your soul as a transference of energy, so to speak. It's a way of clearing your path to ultimate success.

Negativity, betrayal, and darkness can push us into the light of our purpose. I've dealt with my fair share of negativity in this business. When I first arrived in Los Angeles, I was young, naïve, and, dare I say, ignorant to the realities of this business, the sometimes-dark underbelly of the entertainment industry. I had no idea that people could be so devilish in the city of Angels!

The truth is, while Hollywood is glamorous, the lights and action attract a lot of broken people, who assume that fame will heal their wounds and deep-rooted traumas. I've come to learn to take nothing personally, remembering that how people treat you is a reflection of how they feel about themselves. I have also learned that people will drag you into their storms and blame you for the rain. And that's why I always carry an umbrella of protection against life's elements, through prayer.

Instead of dragging *you* through a series of negative situations I've overcome to prove my point, I'd much rather turn to science and the galaxy above. The most beautiful and brightest star that humans have ever discovered is the supernova, but what many don't realize is that supernovas only come into being at the final phase of their lives through exploding—ending in a beautiful light show within the galaxy. As it turns out, supernovas are some of the most violent events in the universe, and the force from the explosion generates blinding flashes of radiation and sends shock waves throughout the galaxy. Simply put, according to science, one thing has to end—explode, even—for something even greater to emerge.

I am in no way asking you, the reader, to willfully place yourself in violent, explosive, or negative situations to become your greatest self. What I am suggesting is, when opposition meets you at your door, welcome it into your home, understanding that the transformative power of negativity has the ability to change your life for the better.

Keep an open mind as we unpack this eighth secret. Not as obvious of a principle to mastering becoming the star of your own life as courage or optimism, negativity plays a principal role in our journey to purpose. Let's examine what good can come of it and explore what can be gained.

Born Calvin Cordozar Broadus Jr., his mother gave him his nickname because she thought he resembled Snoopy from the *Peanuts* cartoon. Snoop shared with me that he had a cousin who named him Tate Doggy Dog, but the name didn't stick, much to his dislike. "When I decided to rename myself Snoop Doggy Dogg, my cousin Tate didn't like it very much, but I promised him, 'I'm gonna take this name to the stars.'"[3] **And that he did.**

Raised in his local Baptist church in Long Beach, Golgotha Trinity, Snoop was a member of the choir where he sang and played piano, helping to cultivate his musical talents.[4] Inspired by the early pioneers of hip-hop like Slick Rick, Kurtis Blow, and Sugarhill Gang, **Snoop took on rapping in the sixth grade, testing and perfecting the lyrical flow that would**

one day dominate airwaves around the world. He penned his first song, "Super Rhymes," and performed it for his classmates. The overwhelming positive response to his gift gave him a brief glimpse into his future, and the possibilities therein.[5]

Snoop was an exemplary athlete, astute student, and dedicated son who bagged groceries and delivered newspapers in the neighborhood to make ends meet and support his mother. He graduated high school with a promising future, but after being rumored to be associated with the wrong crowds in the Rollin' 20 Crips Gang, he soon found himself arrested and locked up for drug possession. Even when locked up, he never stopped rapping and honing his craft. Ironically, his prison mates encouraged him to do away with a life of crime, pushing him to seriously pursue his dream to rap professionally. Their positive reinforcement helped place Snoop on a straight and narrow path.[6]

Whoever could have foreseen that "negative" circumstances would become the impetus that pushed Snoop in a new direction?!

With a new lease on life, post-release from the county jail, he formed a rap and R & B trio called 213 with friends Nate Dogg and Warren G. They became local successes, selling over five hundred tapes out of the trunk of their car, which brought them to the attention of Dr. Dre. He invited Snoop to audition and then brought him on as his main collaborator on Dre's multiplatinum-selling debut solo album, *The Chronic*.

Noted for his distinctive and smooth rap flow, Snoop quickly rose to fame. But no matter how high his star was rising, it seemed as though the gravity of street life would always be there to pull him back down. As Snoop sat in the driver's seat of his Jeep, an argument broke out between his friend McKinley "Malik" Lee and known gang member

Philip Woldermariam. Shots were fired, Woldermariam was shot and killed, and Snoop found himself driving what became the getaway car. After going into hiding for three days, Snoop turned himself in and was charged with first-degree murder.[7]

During the trial, Snoop released a short film and album, *Murder Was the Case*, which debuted on the Billboard 200 and the R & B/hip-hop chart at No. 1, powered by first-week sales of over three hundred thousand copies.[8] A week later, the project was certified Gold, and halfway through the trial reached double platinum, amassing over two million sales. The massive success of the project made Snoop even more of a target for prosecutors during the high-profile trial. But after enlisting the services of famed OJ Simpson lawyer Johnnie Cochran, Snoop was acquitted of all charges. It was through this incredibly negative experience that Snoop was able to find the light within. Following the acquittal, he made a vow to stop rapping about murder and glamorizing the gangster life, and of course this was to the disappointment of his fans, friends, and foes. He chose to redirect his pen's focus to writing about life and all of the good it had to offer.

Three decades later, his commitment to change, brought on by negative circumstances, has proven to be an intelligent and profitable decision. With a multimillion-dollar net worth, Snoop Dogg's business ventures have solidified his position as one of the wealthiest rappers in the game, exemplifying his distinctive business genius. Teaming up with Martha Stewart for a cooking show, developing his own wine label, and even launching a line of dog treats, it's clear Snoop is unstoppable.

WHEN OPPOSITION MEETS
YOU AT YOUR DOOR,
WELCOME IT INTO YOUR
HOME, UNDERSTANDING
THAT THE TRANSFORMATIVE
POWER OF NEGATIVITY HAS
THE ABILITY TO CHANGE
YOUR LIFE FOR THE BETTER.

I had the pleasure of meeting and working with Snoop on his faith-based project, *Bible of Love*, a gospel album, with which he further leaned into his commitment to positivity. He debuted the project on our Hollywood Confidential stage as the *sole* interview during the promotional campaign, walking us through each song with joy and excitement. When I asked him, "Why a gospel project?" he simply said, "I did my share of bringing dark moments. Now it's time to bring the light." In that moment you could feel the energy in the room shift from speculation and judgment to acceptance and understanding. The prodigal son was returning home. He further revealed that he'd promised his mother he'd do a project that she could enjoy, void of profanity and negativity, and he kept his promise. Partnering with some of the biggest names in faith-based music, the project shot to the top of Billboard's Top Gospel Albums Chart, where it debuted at No. 1. Snoop's story truly is a testament to the power of negativity and moving from darkness into light.

I'm so proud to have been part of an amazing campaign and part of history with an artist who has meant so much to so many people around the world. I've been so blessed to break bread with my heroes. But I know I wouldn't have made it this far if I hadn't been shaped by my struggles, and by the dark moments in my life.

I tend to think of success as a seed. A seed has never germinated within the light of day. It must be planted deep down in soil, which contains the proper conditions to bring out the best in the seed, ensuring it sprouts and breaks ground in due time. Similarly, we all have seeds down inside of us, many of which will never be fully actualized until we go through a trying season. With that in mind, I want to thank every person who has betrayed me—every person who has thrown dirt on my name, and every person whose actions have brought me to the dark places in my life. You have been my greatest teachers, helping me ascend to higher heights and deeper depths. You tried to bury me, but it turns out, I was a seed.

I encourage you to reframe negativity, roadblocks, and challenges as a sign that you are on the right path. Where there's resistance, you're preparing for breakthrough. So if you've been buried in darkness, and you're not yet seeing the light of day, I want you to *keep going, and keep growing.* Your greatest opposition signals that your miracle is on the way! Locked up inside the number eight spot on my list of secrets to becoming the star of your own life, this has been a lesson from the word *negativity.*

THREE WAYS

TO TRANSFORM *NEGATIVITY*

BECOME A SEED

When things in your life seem dark, and when circumstances seem overwhelming, almost burying you alive, don't forget, you're a seed. You can rise above it!

SHIFT YOUR PERSPECTIVE

When we go through dark times, it's imperative that we maintain a positive outlook. A quick shift in our perspective can better help us to understand that dark moments in our lives present opportunities for growth. What part of your perspective needs to shift today?

TRUST THE PROCESS OF TRANSFORMATION

When we look to nature, we find several powerful examples of trusting life's process of transformation, but none more so than the process of metamorphosis. When a caterpillar becomes fully grown, it suspends itself under a branch, or at times buries itself underground, inside its silk cocoon for thirty days or more. Some species have been known to endure this process for two full years. Through the process of metamorphosis, the caterpillar then emerges from its cocoon as a beautiful and fully transformed butterfly. Trust the process.

QUESTIONS
for Reflection

How have dark times that I've endured helped to develop my character?

In what ways can I turn my negative experiences into tools that aid my success?

Are there any areas in my life that may have temporarily fallen apart, that can possibly come back together for the better?

Who are the people who have been strategically cast in my life to help me ascend to the next level?

What are the things I can work on within myself while I'm buried away in my metamorphic process?

AFFIRMATION
for Negativity

I UNDERSTAND AND ACCEPT THAT ALTHOUGH PAINFUL, betrayal can be an essential part of my ascension to the next level in my life. Every person I meet, good or bad, has a significant role to play in the growth of my soul. And I hereby give them permission to play their part to the best of their abilities, for my greater good.

Secret # 9 :
TENACITY

"ALMOST MORE THAN TALENT YOU
NEED TENACITY, AND AN INFINITE
CAPACITY FOR REJECTION,
IF YOU ARE TO SUCCEED."

—LARRY KRAMER

W ho put a billboard up on Santa Monica Boulevard for this TV show?"

That first record-breaking docuseries I produced was called *Black Love*. And while we were thankful that the Oprah Winfrey Network picked up the series for four episodes, we actually had a total of eight locked and loaded in the cannon! When we received the news that they only picked up four, I said to myself, "I'm going to create an outdoor campaign that will blow OWN out of the water!" With an independent budget, we secured billboards, benches, and transit ads with subways, trains, and buses to help us evangelize about our upcoming series in ten key markets across the country. One thing about Oprah Winfrey is, she doesn't do off-channel marketing, because she doesn't have to! She *is* the draw. So, when executives from her offices rolled by our outdoor marketing efforts in surprise, I received a call asking, "Who put a billboard up on Santa Monica Boulevard?"

That's how I roll.

Because of the excitement and buzz we created surrounding the little docuseries that could, we broke records, becoming the biggest unscripted show to debut in OWN's history. They purchased the remaining four episodes, and that was the start of a beautiful relationship between me and the Oprah Winfrey Network (thank you to Tina Perry, Tara Montgomery, Brian Piotrowicz, Sheereen Russell, and Fatima Wesley for always seeing, supporting, and championing me).

When our paths crossed on that rooftop in Hollywood, and Oprah refused my thanks, citing the fact that I had done the work to earn the moment, the billboard on Santa Monica Boulevard was evidence of my *tenacity*.

Tenacity is the relentless pursuit that shifts dreams into reality. It will take sheer tenacity—a fierce blend of persistence, resolve, determination, and grit—to become the stars of our own lives.

When unexpected deterrents show up in your life and threaten your plans, how do you handle them? When faced with rejection, do you fight, or do you fold? When your dreams seem impossible to reach, do you give up, or do you build a ladder?

Tenacity has long been the secret formula within the successes of so many iconic personalities, leaders, and global franchises. Can you imagine life without a Frappuccino or vanilla latte from Starbucks? After 217 of the 242 investors founder Howard Schultz talked to rejected his pitch, that was almost the case! But Schultz was relentless in pursuit of his vision and made it happen. Schultz demonstrated tenacity.[1]

And what would life be without our iPhones, MacBook Pros, and a sturdy set of noise-canceling AirPods? I shudder to think. Apple was a leading manufacturer of software, but after the market became over-saturated, they suffered a twelve-year drought. Severely in the red and headed full steam into bankruptcy, Apple rehired Steve Jobs to rebrand the company, as failure was not an option. After researching consumer needs, Jobs restructured the company and helped Apple become one of the biggest, most successful companies in the world![2] The company demonstrated tenacity.

Finally, what would you think about a world without light bulbs? Sounds pretty dim to me. In comes Thomas Edison, a young inventor credited with engineering the electric light bulb, but not before failing to

"I HAVE NOT FAILED TEN THOUSAND TIMES, I'VE SUCCESSFULLY FOUND TEN THOUSAND WAYS THAT WILL NOT WORK."

—THOMAS EDISON

do so over thousands of well-documented attempts. While many deemed him a failure throughout his many unsuccessful efforts, he simply said, "I have not failed ten thousand times, I've successfully found ten thousand ways that will not work."[3] Edison was fiercely tenacious.

These are all tangible glimpses of tenacity in action. It's that grit and perseverance that kicks into overdrive when it seems that all hope is lost. It's never quitting, even when the road gets rough. It's a character trait that we all possess but few harness—instead, many opt to accept defeat just before the sweet taste of victory. In the words of Edison, "Many of life's failures are people who did not realize how close they were to success when they gave up."[4]

While Edison did not have this group in mind, those who come to LA to make it in the business can be among those who are tempted to give up without realizing how close they might have been to success. But I get it. Rejection is a natural and ever-present part of the business of Hollywood. I'm constantly pitching ideas to studios, networks, and corporations to greenlight my ideas, which are more often than not met with *no*. But as the saying goes, rejection is simply redirection, leading us down our destined paths.

When I first started Hollywood Confidential, there were many supporters—certainly enough for us to launch—but also many who didn't believe in it. We pushed past the doubters and created a brand that grossed over $500,000 in sponsorship annually, and we were slated to have our biggest year yet. But out of nowhere came the silent killer: *the pandemic.* I lost over $750,000 in committed sponsorships for the brand and TV show concepts I had sold. We were no longer able to do live events or produce TV shows, as the entertainment industry came to a standstill.

Instead of folding, I came up with ways to sustain myself through creating passive streams of income that couldn't be impacted by unexpected natural disasters. That tenacity afforded me the opportunity to produce the J.Lo video at the end of 2020—with most of the crew wearing COVID masks—diversifying my production services, as I had never done music videos before. But at the end of the day, I had to eat. After securing that opportunity, I got serious about securing my book deal. Next up, I secured a podcast production deal for Hollywood Confidential with media titan Charles D. King through his three-time Oscar Award-winning production company, Macro. What I've learned in this game of life is that tenacity wants to win, and it lives by the creed that failure is not an option. When failure lurks at our door, tenacity answers, declaring, "I will not lose!"

One of those tenacious winners is Tyler Perry, a self-made billionaire who is a world-renowned producer, director, actor, screenwriter, playwright, entrepreneur, philanthropist, and two-time *New York Times* bestselling author. His brainchild, Tyler Perry Studios, is headquartered in Atlanta, consisting of twelve sound stages that span 330 acres. The complex is bigger than Disney, Warner Brothers, and Paramount Studios combined. Celebrated among the pantheon of today's greatest cinematic innovators, his unique blend of spiritual hope and down-home humor continues to shape his inspiring life story, connecting with fans across the globe and always leaving space to dream.

Truly a beacon of hope and inspiration to many, Tyler Perry is tenacity personified. His personal story, although laced with tragedy, is one of the most awe-inspiring testaments to the power of persistence, full of lessons that can be applied by all who are in pursuit of landing their dreams.

Born Emmitt Perry Jr. in New Orleans, Louisiana, Tyler grew up in a severely abusive household. He recollects that his father's answer to everything was to beat it out of you. After enduring years of physical and sexual abuse at the hands of those meant to protect him, he saw suicide as his only way out of torment.[5] Unsuccessfully attempting to take his life multiple times, he found the inner pain and turmoil in his life unbearable,[6] but a chance encounter with a media maven would turn out to be the intervention he needed. One day while watching *The Oprah Winfrey Show*, he heard her say that writing down one's experiences can be cathartic. "After I found a dictionary and looked up 'cathartic,'" Perry said, "I realized what she was saying, so I started writing." He described unearthing memories that he called "God's little flashes of light." And that's when his writing career began.[7]

The pages of his journal then morphed into his first stage play, *I Know I've Been Changed*. Having saved $12,000, he rented a local theater in Atlanta to house the production, and to his dismay, only thirty people showed up over the play's run. Never one to quit, over the course of six long years, Perry continued to hone his craft as a playwright, while unsuccessfully attempting to stage his production. During this tedious and seemingly unrewarding process, he faced nearly insurmountable obstacles, endured financial distress, and even braved homelessness, all in pursuit of his dreams. Deciding to give it one more try, Perry's persistence finally paid off. Word had begun to spread across Atlanta about his stage play, and it ended up selling out for an eight-night run! When the show was moved from a smaller venue into Atlanta's renowned Fox Theater, the *Washington Post* gave it a favorable review, and the same Hollywood that had rejected him years prior came calling.[8] Signing a multimillion-dollar deal with Lionsgate and creating a successful portfolio of content over the last twenty years as a writer, producer, and director has done Tyler well, positioning him as a true titan and anomaly within the entertainment industry.

Now he's the craftsman behind twenty-four feature films, twenty stage plays, and seventeen television shows (at the time of writing this book); it's clear that Hollywood originally underestimated Tyler's ability to connect with a niche audience that had been severely underserved and ignored. They also underestimated his level of tenacity. Tyler never let rejection, criticism, obstacles, or challenges deter him from pursuing his dream.

One of my longtime dreams was to work with Tyler in a creative capacity, and it finally happened for me. WACO—which stands for Where Art Can Occur—is dedicated to the empowerment of Los Angeles artists, young people, and stories of the African diaspora. The event I produced for them in 2019—my first sold show!—was called **OWN Presents: Inside WACO's Wearable Art Gala.** To have Tyler as a participant in one of my creative works was an honor. Hearing him record adverts about my concept was music to my ears, an experience I won't soon forget, and one of the greatest rewards that tenacity has brought my way.

On this journey to becoming the star of your own life you *will* face obstacles that require persistence, resolve, determination, and grit. Maybe you've sent out thirty resumes and haven't yet gotten one interview. Maybe you've struggled to pay for the degree or certification you need to take your next step. Or you might just be having trouble finding a reliable babysitter you can trust to free up your time to finally write that bestselling novel. My friend, I am convinced that you have what it takes to make your dream a reality, but no one else is going to do it for you. You have to keep showing up, one day at a time, stepping into the unknown. You might be scared, broke, or both—and I get it, it can feel like your world is caving in. But the worst thing you can do is give up on yourself when life gets hard. You are worth the grit. When you practice tenacity, when you find creative solutions to the problems you're facing, when you carve a new path around the obstacle in your way, you will reach your dreams.

Sitting divine at number nine of my list of secrets to becoming the star of your own life is *tenacity*.

FIVE WAYS

TO CULTIVATE *TENACITY*

SET YOUR GOALS

Understanding your objectives and what motivates you is paramount when it comes to cultivating tenacity. Create a list of the things you want to achieve, and how you want your life to look, and then set out to accomplish them by any means necessary!

START WHERE YOU ARE

Many times, we delay endeavoring on our ideas because we don't have the resources, or the timing doesn't feel right. But when we take a leap of faith and do the best we can with what we've got, we will attract the right situations and opportunities into our lives to help us grow as we go. Wherever you are standing today, what is one tenacious step forward you can take?

KNOW YOUR WORTH

Understanding the value of what you bring to the table is a game changer, and an essential factor in developing a tenacious mindset. When what you have is a commodity, then you know it's worth fighting for. As the saying goes, know your worth and then add tax! This might be dollars, or it might be a trade of services, but spend time writing and reflecting on the *value* of what you're bringing.

BE RESILIENT

If at first you don't succeed, dust yourself off and try again, and again, and again if you have to! The art of bouncing back after failure or rejection is key when it comes to living tenaciously. Failure can be looked at as a stepping stone to future success. Learn to accept failure as an open invitation to try again, and this time, with the lessons accrued from past experience. What is the most recent failure from which you are dusting yourself off? Is there a way in which this failure can serve you as a stepping stone to the next thing?

BE RELENTLESS

Be willing to work tirelessly to achieve your dreams. Do something every single day that gets you closer to your desired outcome. And when you've run out of opportunities to explore, create your own! What is one opportunity that you can seize, or create, today?

QUESTIONS
for Reflection

What are the specific ways that practicing tenacity can help me build a bridge to reaching my dreams?

Are there any dreams I've had that I gave up on too soon? And how might I pick them back up today?

What are the goals and objectives that are driving me to want to succeed?

How can I better power through the pain of rejection to receive my desired outcome in life? What practical strategies will I use?

What is the way, or ways, that I am using fear of failure as an excuse that hinders me from pursuing the life of my dreams?

AFFIRMATION
for Tenacity

THE STEEL OF MY RESOLVE GRACES ME WITH TENACITY, grants me endurance, and assures me of ultimate success. By standing firm on my objectives and goals, and refusing to fold in the face of rejection, I cultivate a mindset of unwavering perseverance. I call in divine assistance from the four corners of the world to assist me in achieving my goals. I will not fail.

Secret #10:

INTENTIONALITY

"INTENTION IS A CONSCIOUS CHOICE
FROM WITHIN AND THE MINDFUL
EXERCISING OF THAT CHOICE.
INTENTION IS PERSONAL ACTIVISM
IN ALIGNMENT WITH OUR DEEPEST,
MOST PEACEFUL TRUTH AND
OUR HIGHEST PURPOSE FOR OUR
GREATEST GOOD. IT IS THE CONSCIOUS
CREATION OF A SOULFUL LIFE."

—ADRIENNE ENNS

f we're keeping it one hundred, I don't think Beyoncé became the biggest star in the world because she's the most beautiful, the most talented, or the hardest worker. And if you think so, then you're *big* wrong.

Now that I have your attention, you may be asking yourself, "Is Steve crazy?" And to that, I say, possibly! But before you put this book down in protest—talent, beauty, and work ethic aside, may I submit to you the proposition that Beyoncé's ascendance to the top of the solar system is solely due to the power of intentionality, which is the tenth confidential secret to becoming the star of your own life.

Intentionality brings us closer to our dreams. The things that bring us joy, bring us fulfillment, and give us purpose—they are in our reach, but only if we consciously act to achieve them.

Of all of the entertainers I've had the pleasure of working with, no one is more centered inside their purpose on the world's stage than Beyoncé Giselle Knowles. With over twenty-five years of dominating airwaves, topping Billboard charts, and shifting the cultural landscape of entertainment, Beyoncé continues to elevate her craft, proving to the world she's that girl. She's successfully rewritten the rules of album releases, visual companion pieces, and world tours, while singlehandedly redefining the future of the music industry—and doing so with grace and ease. Amassing a fortune nearing a billion dollars[1] in the worlds of music, movies, fashion, and the beauty industry, her legacy is forever woven into the fabric of American history. The most decorated Grammy winner in history,[2] with an impenetrable work ethic and legions of adoring fans, Beyoncé easily sits atop the list of the greatest entertainers of all time.

Paying homage to my former marketing career, this chapter will read like a case study, where we will examine the success of Beyoncé. And at the end of our investigation, we will once again apply our findings to the journey of becoming the stars of our very own lives. Let's get into it, shall we?

FIVE WAYS BEYONCÉ USED THE POWER OF INTENTIONALITY TO BECOME THE BIGGEST STAR IN THE WORLD

BETTING ON HERSELF

Hailing from the Lone Star State, Beyoncé is proof that everything in Texas *is* bigger. She developed a strong work ethic at a young age, taking dance classes, entering local talent shows, and performing solos with her church choir. At the age of nine, she and her childhood friends formed the group Girl's Tyme—later called Destiny's Child—which went on to become the biggest-selling female group of all time, boasting over fifty million albums sold worldwide.[3]

But consider this: At the height of the group's success, Beyoncé made a high-stakes, yet *intentional*, risk, in deciding to leave the group in search of her own personal destiny as a solo artist. That's bold, right? Betting on herself paid off. To date, Beyoncé is one of the highest paid women in the music industry at large, amassing an impressive musical catalog that has spanned over three decades. No risk, no reward.

BEING UNPREDICTABLE

Beyoncé remains unclockable! You never know how, or when, but you can guarantee she will deliver, but in her *own* time. She is intentional with *her* timing, and she's not concerned about doing things the way they've always been done. She's mastered the art of unpredictability, as best displayed in her surprise visual album. With no marketing, no promotional campaign, and no lead single, Beyoncé pulled the biggest surprise in modern-day music by secretly releasing her album at midnight on December 13, 2013. She made all fourteen tracks exclusively available on iTunes all at one time, with accompanying visuals to match.

She stopped the world! A monumental and global event, the Beyoncé album instantaneously became the fastest-selling project in iTunes history, shooting to No. 1 in over one hundred countries, cementing Beyoncé's place in music history as one of the most daring, unpredictable, and revolutionary artists of all time.

Forever changing the mechanics of how musicians connect directly with consumers on their product, Beyoncé continues to be intentional in using the strategy of unpredictability to maintain visibility in this industry. The *Renaissance* album. Global tours. And the 2024 Super Bowl announcement of her debut country project, *Cowboy Carter,* by way of dropping two surprise singles and topping the charts overnight. How's that for unpredictability? As a result, she's made history again, becoming the first Black female artist to ever reach the top of the Apple Music US Country charts.[4]

Quite frankly, we love to see it.

NO INTERVIEWS, PLEASE

Interviews with major publications, radio, and talk shows have traditionally reigned supreme within the hierarchy of an artist's strategy to remain relevant. Not so much for Beyoncé, who flat-out stopped giving interviews in 2013, without explanation. Doubling down on her efforts, she sent shockwaves through the industry in 2015 when she notoriously decided to withhold a Q&A for her cover story and subsequent feature for *Vogue*.[5] And outside of my interview in 2019 (smile) she has issued virtually *no* TV interviews.

Understanding the law of supply and demand, Beyoncé continues to prove that less is more. This is intentionality at work! Her ability to trend above the headlines demonstrates the fact that she alone *is* the interview, the visual, and the perpetual moment.

SOCIALLY UNSOCIAL

Most celebrities use social media for the continued exposure and expansion of their brands by providing direct access and engagement to their fans and target consumers. Meanwhile, Beyoncé has made an intentional decision to socially unplug. When she does decide to post images, at her leisure, she does so without accompanying captions, virtually sending the internet into a frenzy. By detaching from social media altogether, she's actually mastered it. (Sound familiar? See chapter 6.)

Through practicing boundaries by refusing to offer the intimate details of her personal life for public consumption, she's given fans no choice but to feast upon the art, which in turn serves as the nutrients that keep the Beyoncé brand vital, healthy, and strong.

In her own words, "We live in a world with few boundaries and a lot of access. There are so many internet therapists, comment critics, and experts with no expertise. Our reality can be warped because it's based on a personalized algorithm. It shows us whatever truths we are searching for, and that's dangerous." She continued, "We can create our own false reality when we're not fed a balance of what's truly going on in the world. It's easy to forget that there's still so much to discover outside of our phones. I'm grateful I have the ability to choose what I want to share. One day I decided I wanted to be like Sade and Prince. I wanted the focus to be on my music, because if my art isn't strong enough or meaningful enough to keep people interested and inspired, then I'm in the wrong business. My music, my films, my art, my message—that should be enough."[6]

KEEPING IT IN-HOUSE

Complete ownership of your brand is essential when it comes to becoming the biggest star in the world. A quiet storm, Parkwood Entertainment reportedly generates over $12 million a year.[7] Expanding well beyond music, the company Beyoncé built houses departments in video production, management, marketing, digital, creative, philanthropy, and publicity.

Over the last decade, we've seen Parkwood spearhead initiatives such as BeyGOOD, Beyoncé's foundation that creates opportunities for marginalized communities and businesses of color. Signing, launching, and managing the careers of Grammy-nominated duo Chloe x Halle; producing the cultural phenomenon known as the Renaissance Tour (grossing over $500 million worldwide)[8] and subsequent documentary film that debuted in AMC theaters; and most recently, developing and launching her long-awaited hair-care line, Cécred!

Proving to be one of the most lucrative business decisions she's ever made, the formation of Parkwood only further speaks to the brilliance and intentionality of Beyoncé. She's doing it her way, by keeping it *all in-house*.

I love a good case study! As you can see, Beyoncé's success hasn't occurred by happenstance but rather by intention. Through embracing risk, avoiding predictability, maintaining firm boundaries, making strategic decisions, and taking full control over her vision, she's been able to dominate the entertainment industry as one of the biggest icons the world of pop culture has ever witnessed.

I'm grateful to have been able to work with such a force—first at the genesis of my career, which allowed me to witness history in the making, and again at a critical time in my career when I had everything to prove as a first-time creator and the executive producer of **OWN Presents: Inside WACO's Wearable Art Gala** primetime special. Her contributions to my life have truly been the gifts that have kept on giving. Thank you, Beyoncé, for being a beautiful teacher to me and so many others.

This year, I will celebrate fifteen years in the city of Los Angeles. I couldn't have made it without the support of my loving family, the best tribe I could have ever assembled, and the power of intentional living. Early on in my LA journey, I decided to create a mission statement, to ensure that any opportunity that came my way was aligned with the person I wanted to become. My statement read, "My mission is to inspire and empower people around the world to reach their highest potential and to live their dreams through education, mentorship, and integrity-based principles and practices." Here I am, doing more of that. That's the power of intention.

Let's be intentional about being intentional. Embrace risk. You'll determine what "risk" looks like for you and what degree of risk you're willing to accommodate. Maybe you'll use most of your savings to record an album. Maybe you'll purchase booth space at an upcoming festival to sell your product. Or you might do what I did, by leaving the comfort of home to journey to the place where your dreams can be realized. Be intentional when it comes to embracing the right risk.

Be unpredictable. Keeping your plans close to your chest prohibits outside interference from sabotaging your dreams. It also keeps supporters and onlookers engaged, on the edge of their seats, wanting more. Don't oversaturate the marketplace with your presence. Give just enough, at the right time and frequency, to make an impact, and keep them coming back for more!

Develop boundaries. Be clear on what you will and won't do when it comes to achieving your very own success. Once you're clear on the nonnegotiables of you, it's important to then defend those boundaries, prioritizing your deepest desires above all else. Lean into the knowledge and belief that you are worthy of your own advocacy. When you establish your goals and devote yourself to protecting them, you can become the master of your fate.

Be strategic. Strategy is a huge part of being intentional. It's not only asking, "*How* are we going to do this?" but also, "Why?" The world expected Beyoncé to post on social, Oprah to continue her TV show, and J.Lo to stay in her lane dancing—but each was strategic about when and how they moved. Whether you're a creative, a business executive, or the single parent of a toddler, you don't have to do what's expected. You can create success on your very own terms by implementing your own unique strategy for success.

Maintain ownership. I'm encouraging you to be thoughtful about ownership of whatever it is that you make, build, design, produce, or develop. While there are situations in which it makes sense to partner with others to execute your vision, it may also be strategic for you to maintain ownership of what you're offering the world.

Living intentionally has allowed me to create a life I like to live. My story and the stories within the pages of this book are living proof that we can truly do anything we put our minds to, as long as we are willing to do the work required. Keeping in mind that success is not one size fits all, intentionality is likely going to look different for you than it does for someone else. So be thoughtful and strategic in how you wield it.

Charting at number ten on my playlist of secrets to becoming the star of your own life is a tune called *intentionality*—likened to the track you skipped over but later found out was fire. And if you'd like to find practical ways to incorporate the melody of intention into the song of your life, then find the "sheet music" on the following pages.

FOUR WAYS

TO PRACTICE BEING *INTENTIONAL*

CREATE A MISSION STATEMENT

Develop a personal mission statement based on your purpose and core principles. Affirming your mission in life only helps to ensure that you are taking the necessary steps that help align you with the person you desire to become. Never forget that intentionality happens by action! Spend time this week crafting a mission statement.

ELIMINATE DISTRACTIONS

Practice unplugging from social media, your cellular devices, and any other methods of communication that can cause you to become distracted from your goals. Mindful consumption is the key. Get serious about shortening the distance between your dreams and reality! This week, unplug from socials and notice what happens inside you. (Repeat as necessary.)

LEARN TO SAY NO

When you're good at so many things, your participation and input become invaluable within the lives of so many. And while being needed by loved ones feels great, your goals and dreams need you just the same. Practice saying no, and repurpose the energy you give out into building the life you deserve. Over the next four weeks, pay attention to the "asks" you receive, and try to say no to the ones that aren't for you.

SET CLEAR BOUNDARIES

It's been said that givers have to set limits because takers never will. Be aware of who and what is taking time away from your goals and be willing to set healthy boundaries around your sacred time. We only have twenty-four hours in a day. Seven of those are devoted to sleep, and another eight are devoted to our jobs. If we want to be intentional in reaching our dreams, it is imperative that we safeguard our time by implementing healthy boundaries in order to distribute it accordingly. This week, mark your calendar with the hours during which you will be intentional about taking steps to become the star of your own life.

QUESTIONS
for Reflection

In a world full of distractions, how can I learn to be more present? List specific actions you'll take to be present to the present.

How can I practice being more intentional, in order to better reach my goals? Create three action items you'll execute this week to reach your goals.

In what areas of my life can I practice being my own advocate? Spend time reflecting and journaling on this one.

What are the things in my life that matter most? What changes do I need to make to prioritize these?

In what areas of my life can I practice placing healthy boundaries in order to be successful?

AFFIRMATION *for Intentionality*

WHEN I MOVE WITH INTENTION, I ALIGN MYSELF WITH my greatest good and consciously create a soulful life. Through welcoming the awareness of intention, I lovingly place a spotlight on my purpose and the things that matter most to me. As I drown out distractions, and prioritize my deepest desires, I find it easier to place boundaries around my time, my energy, and my essence. I am worthy of my own advocacy and worthy of living the life of my dreams.

Secret #11:
AUTHENTICITY

"AUTHENTICITY IS A COLLECTION OF CHOICES THAT WE HAVE TO MAKE EVERY DAY. IT'S ABOUT THE CHOICE TO SHOW UP AND BE REAL. THE CHOICE TO BE HONEST. THE CHOICE TO LET OUR TRUE SELVES BE SEEN."

—BRENÉ BROWN

When the Black Lives Matter movement began to gain momentum, several people I respect in the industry warned me to not speak out publicly, suggesting that it could end my career. They believed that I could be penalized by the gatekeepers for speaking my truth.

I've always had a strong conviction about what's right and what's wrong and have, more often than not, found myself happily advocating for the underdog. So I thought about it, considered the costs, and decided that the opportunity to advocate on behalf of marginalized communities outweighed any repercussions that could come as a result. In that historic moment, I not only helped to organize a few marches and rallies with prominent entertainers in Hollywood, but I also made the conscious decision to use my social media platforms to educate and inform followers and non-followers alike on implicit bias, systemic racism, and criminal justice reform.

While there's no way to calculate what professional opportunities I may have lost, I did lose a lot of followers on social media. And I gained some as well. But since that time my Instagram page has been suppressed, reaching only a fraction of the followers it reached prior to speaking out. Even still, I'll never regret making a decision to publicly advocate on behalf of the voiceless. And I'll never regret speaking out against what I feel is wrong. Even if it comes at a cost, my integrity is not for sale.

I'm a disruptor, and that's not always a welcome trait or characteristic. But it's one of the principal roles I was cast to play on the world's stage and within the lives of those I've been divinely assigned to collide with. While it's been tempting to go with the flow or stay silent, that's not who I am or who I was uniquely created to be. Above all, I have learned the power and importance of being myself, as every other role has already been taken.

It took a few years and tough conversations with myself to realize that I am unapologetically and unequivocally meant to be Steve. And that making myself small so as to not intimidate or offend others doesn't serve anyone at all. It is in fact a disservice to the very God who created me. I've come to learn that I am not for everybody, and that's perfectly okay. For when I'm my authentic self, I will attract the people who love me, support me, and embrace me for who I am, just as I am.

I'm convinced that authenticity is the ultimate path to freedom. It's a superpower that aids in saving us from falling ten stories deep into a world full of imposters and pretenders. Authenticity keeps us honest. I'm also a firm believer in the notion that God cannot bless who we pretend to be. Wearing masks disguises our truest, most beautiful selves. So why do we hide? We want acceptance. Society plays a significant role in the suppression of the soul. Life has taught many of us to conform or conceal our true identities out of fear of rejection. So we go along to get along, collecting and clothing ourselves with fragments of fractured identities woven together as protective armor, only to later discover that in doing so, we've inflicted a great deal of self-harm.

In today's society, we see inauthenticity every day in the world of social media, an endless algorithm of inauthentic interactions and facades. Curated highlight reels cascade our explorer pages, drowning us in false imagery, delusions of grandeur, and self-aggrandizing behavior. I honestly believe that if we're not careful, social media will be fully responsible for creating the largest generation of narcissists the world has ever seen. But I digress. We need more critical thinkers who aren't afraid to push against societal norms and stand out from the crowd—especially when we're on a quest to become the stars of our own lives.

The eleventh secret I want to share with you is authenticity. And who better to illustrate this quality than someone *I love*, who happens to be the sheer embodiment of it.

She's the woman who walked into the room, and subsequently my life, with a beautiful smile and warm spirit to match. The first time I met Tabitha Brown—whom many of you know as "America's Mom"—was when she attended one of our workshops for actors. Back in 2015, Hollywood Confidential launched our actors' workshop, a derivative of our large-scale event series, specifically designed to train actors on technique and allow them to showcase in front of some of today's biggest casting directors, agents, and managers.

At that time Tabitha was an up-and-coming aspiring actress, dealing with the hardships and realities of the entertainment industry. But even then, upon meeting her, I knew two things to be true. First, I knew she'd be a star. Some people just have that energy and presence, and Tabitha had it. Second, I knew that our lives would somehow be closely knit together. And today we remain dear friends. Not only is she one of the people who loves me for me, but she doubles as one of the most beautiful examples of authenticity in motion both in my life and on the world's stage.

Out of a class of seventy-five students, that day she was the student who really shined. Her ability to emote, command the space, and tap into a reservoir of emotions caused her to stand out from the crowd. It was clear to everyone in the room that she had a powerful gift that was meant to touch the world. So much so, I wrote about her, in that leather journal that Brandy gave me, that evening after class: "Today, I met an actress who I know will one day become famous. I have so many scripted ideas with an actress of her caliber in mind, and I hope to attach her to a project and *discover* her before someone else makes her a star!"

What none of us in that acting class knew was that Tabitha was suffering from an unexplained autoimmune disease. She had chronic fatigue, blurry vision, and a headache in the back of her head. Excruciating pain was running through her body nonstop, at times rendering her unable to walk. What was worse was, after hundreds of tests, shots in her spine, her head, and steroid medications, doctors were unable to identify her ailment, so she was unable to be properly treated.[1]

After a year and seven months of intolerable pain, Tabitha found herself on the bathroom floor, unable to walk. Through her tears she prayed to God, stating that if he healed her, he could have her life, completely. Soon after, her daughter came home from school and shared her excitement about a documentary she had watched called *What the Health*.[2] As a result, the entire family went on a thirty-day vegan challenge. After the first ten days, Tabitha realized her headache was gone, and by the end of the challenge, her strength had completely returned. Amazed at the results, she continued and made veganism a lifestyle.[3]

A few months into her healing, Tabitha had a dream where she saw herself on a show, but the screen was really small. And because her dreams have always been meaningful to her, she asked God what it meant, and she heard a voice say, "Start doing videos." She knew that meant social media, and she told God, "No, I don't want to do that. I'm not a social media influencer; I'm a professional actress, and I take my career seriously." When God reminded her of their bathroom-floor deal, she protested, answering, "You caught me on a bad day that day."[4]

Committed to living a life of obedience to God, a few months into her healing, she had an idea to begin sharing her journey and vegan recipes online to her then almost nonexistent social media following. I can remember there being thirty of us in her live chats, but we was up in there!

Before launching into this new and exciting digital endeavor, Tabitha felt compelled to lean more into her authentic self, revealing to many of us for the first time that she had a deep Southern drawl, as most people from North Carolina do! But having been told that her accent made her sound ignorant and would serve as a deterrent to landing her dream role, she had chosen to code-switch and covered up her accent in order to make it big in Hollywood. However, almost immediately after committing to embracing her country roots, she hit it big![5]

One day, in between picking up and dropping off Uber customers, she stopped at Whole Foods for lunch, where she discovered the TTLA vegan sandwich. She shared a review online, country accent in tow, and the video went viral, reaching over one million views in a week.[6] Something about her energy and authenticity resonated with digital viewers around the world, and she quickly became a trusted authority on veganism in the hearts and minds of many. She landed her first brand deal with Whole Foods as an ambassador, and the rest is history![7]

When I interviewed Tabitha on our stage at Hollywood Confidential, she spoke candidly on learning to become her authentic self, and the challenges she's experienced throughout the process. "For so long, I did pretend to be someone else, and I did try to fit in. It was like I was telling God, 'You didn't do a good enough job creating me as I am.' When I look back, I was never *not* myself. I've always been the same genuine spirit. But I did succumb to the pressure to fit in. And it was suffocating me." She continued, "I knew I had to take off the many layers that I had put on to become my authentic self. I realized that by suppressing who I was—by code-switching, by covering my accent, and by straightening my hair—I wasn't free. And we were born to be free! And so now I'm on my freedom walk. But to be fully transparent, sometimes in certain environments I get triggered and deal with a little PTSD, but I have to remind myself that I no longer have to conform. It's still a journey, but I'm worth it. We all are."[8]

And what a journey it has been! To date, Tabitha has amassed a collective social media following of over ten million strong! She is a three-time *New York Times* bestselling author, she launched her very own hair-care line in ULTA Beauty named Donna's Recipe, her very own seasoning blends with McCormick, and a massively successful capsule collection with Target—spanning food, homeware, and clothing! And most recently, she won her first Emmy Award for hosting her children's show, *Tab Time*, a program created to reach and inspire the next generation of dreamers.

Gatekeepers in any industry (and some people in the comments section on social media) might pressure you to hide or disguise who you are. The industry told Tabitha that speaking in her natural voice, with that signature country accent, meant that she would be viewed as less intelligent, or as a country bumpkin, and that there was no way it would translate into mainstream success. So, for a minute, she masked her Southern twang to appeal to the mainstream. But look at the amazing things that happened for her when she embraced her authentic self!

So whether it's your voice, your skin, or something else that is altogether true to who you are, I'm challenging you to lean into what makes you uniquely you. And that's because I am convinced that being your authentic self is how you're going to *win* at being the star of your own life. No matter what lane you're in, you'll face some kind of temptation to dial back who you truly are. But I want to encourage you to spend some time considering what authenticity is going to look like for you on your journey. For me, it meant having the courage to speak my truth, knowing I could suffer consequences for staying true to myself. For my friend Tabitha, it meant refusing to code-switch and using her natural inflection. For you, it might look like finding the strength to leave a relationship (romantically, professionally, or platonically) that no longer works for the person you are today. We all change and evolve, and, contrary to popular belief, we don't have to commit long-term to playing a role that no longer serves us. Some contracts are meant to be broken, especially ones that can bring about pain, impede our progress, and cause us to lose the essence of who we intrinsically are.

I'm also challenging you to spend some time considering the ways in which you can bring your fully authentic self to the world, as the benefits to authentic living are bountiful, leading to abundance and fulfillment untold. Lovingly landing at the number eleven spot on my list of secrets to becoming the star of your own life is *authenticity*. And if you're looking to become more of your authentic self in order to maximize your purpose, you're in luck, as I've assembled seven ways to help you embrace your truest self.

SIX WAYS

TO EMBRACE *AUTHENTICITY*

DON'T BE EASILY INFLUENCED

It's easy to allow our friends or family to influence our decisions, and societal norms often do play a role in the suppression of the soul. Instead of conforming to the norm, make a conscious decision to stand out as your own individual self. This week, notice the specific ways that friends and family pressure you to be other than who you are.

SEEK CLARITY ON WHO YOU ARE

In order to consistently show up as our authentic selves, we must first know who we are. Getting to know ourselves may call for isolation, where we can intentionally create space to get to know ourselves on a deeper level, void of distractions. In the next month, carve out some intentional time to get to know yourself and what brings you joy, as you alone are responsible for your happiness.

BE CONSISTENT

Consistency runs parallel with authenticity. When choosing authenticity, be aware of choices you make consistently in your life. These are an indicator of what comprises your most authentic self. Notice the areas in which you're currently being inconsistent in how you show up in the world. Inconsistency could be a signal that you still have more work to do in living authentically.

SPEAK YOUR TRUTH

Honest communication plays a huge role in authentic living. Becoming comfortable in bringing our whole selves to the table extends an invitation to like-minded individuals to take a seat with us. Never be afraid to speak your truth; your tribe awaits you. Where is the place in your life where you've softened the truth rather than speaking it boldly?

FOLLOW YOUR INTUITION

It's never a bad decision to drown out the noise and distractions of life and home in on the still, small voice inside of us to help guide our decisions. The next time you feel tempted to be influenced by external forces, look within, and look up. The soul always knows. Today, spend twenty minutes—or two minutes!—in purposeful silence. Notice what your intuition is telling you.

BE GENTLE WITH YOURSELF

Once you've decided to move into becoming more of who you authentically are, you may find yourself backsliding into your old habits. The reality is, old habits die hard. And when you've spent a significant portion of your life showing up in a certain way, it serves as a sure means of safety and comfort. In your process of removing the many layers of protection that you've put on, please remember to be gentle with yourself. Authenticity is not a destination, but an ongoing, never-ending journey. What is one way, this week, that you can be gentle with yourself?

QUESTIONS
for Reflection

When do I feel most free to be my honest self? Be specific.

Are there any parts of me that I'm hiding to fit in, and if so, why?

If I were to remove the mask I wear in public, would I like the person staring back at me in the mirror? If yes, why? If not, why not?

In what ways have society and the opinions of others played a role in the suppression of my soul?

Is the collection of choices I'm making on a daily basis leading me to become my most authentic self, and how so (or how not)? Be specific.

AFFIRMATION *for Authenticity*

TODAY, I WILLFULLY REMOVE MY MASK, MAKING A choice to allow the world to see me for who I truly am. I lovingly exchange my need for approval with radical acceptance, and firmly push back against any ideologies that seek to suppress my soul's expression. Authenticity is my one-way ticket to freedom, and I fully give myself permission to take flight.

Secret #12:
LUMINOSITY

"WE ARE STARS WRAPPED IN
SKIN. THE LIGHT YOU ARE SEEKING
HAS ALWAYS BEEN WITHIN."

—RUMI

My favorite hymn in church as a child was called "This Little Light of Mine." The lyrics are, "This little light of mine, I'm gonna let it shine. All around the world, I'm gonna let it shine. Everywhere I go, I'm gonna let it shine. Let it shine, let it shine, let it shine." I loved the idea that not only did I have a powerful light inside of me, but that the possession of that light bestowed on me a great responsibility.

Just like the sky above, I believe that each of us has a galaxy of light within us, shining as bright as the stars in the darkest of nights, illuminating our very souls. The light within us is transformative, and when we share that light, our lives become lighthouses providing guidance and refuge to those in search of a safe place to anchor their vessels. The light we carry has the ability to illuminate the darkest of pathways, serving as a beacon of hope to the world and those around us.

You know that light, that energy, that I noticed the first time I met Tabitha? I was better able to identify and acknowledge the light within her because I had already identified the light within myself. I knew there was something inside of me that spoke to the dream inside of her. And we came together to be of help to each other in our times of need. One thing I know for sure is that we all have our very own measure of luminosity inside of us. To be luminous is to produce or emit light, especially in dark places. The greater the luminosity of an object, the brighter it appears. Just like the lyrics to my favorite hymn, once we have identified the light within, it's our job to cultivate, nourish, protect, and safeguard that light. And then to share it with everyone we come in contact with. When we embrace this responsibility, when we take on the role of being a lighthouse to all those we come in contact with, we grant them a license to be luminous. And together, we light up the world!

Luminosity is the final secret to becoming the star of your own life.

So how bright is your light? Only you can determine the luminosity of your star. Scientifically speaking, the brightness of a star is in direct proportion to the amount of energy it produces. Stars are continuously crushing themselves inward, and the gravitational friction created causes their interiors to heat up. The brighter a star, the hotter its temperature. The hotter the temperature, the brighter the star becomes. This process of nuclear fusion occurring within a star gives off a massive amount of energy and light that shines so brightly, we can see it with our human eyes, even though we're millions of light-years away.

In this beautiful yet sometimes crazy experience called life, we can often find ourselves in predicaments that cause the light within us to fade. But through it all, we have to fight to preserve the integrity of the eternal flame that lives within us. Same as you, I've been faced with many hardships that threatened to exterminate my light. The biggest of those? Not feeling seen. I have dedicated my life's work to creating space and opportunity for marginalized communities and voices to be both seen and heard, while simultaneously feeling overlooked and under-appreciated. Making contributions to the careers of future Emmy, Oscar, and Grammy award–winning creatives without so much as a thank-you or a gesture of appreciation can be mentally, spiritually, and emotion-ally exhausting. Add in the extreme pressures of staying relevant in an ever-changing industry, while sustaining your vision in a competitive and oversaturated market full of people who pretend not to see you while copying your every move, and you'll see why this industry is not for the faint of heart.

But it's in these times that I'm reminded that pressure makes diamonds. And every time I push past disappointment's grasp, deeper into purpose, I'm depositing more fragments of light into the prism of my soul. It's through that process that my light will shine brighter than ever, attracting the right opportunities, experiences, and desired outcomes like moths to a flame. That type of aligned living is greater than any award, accolade, or acknowledgment I could receive. Even if I'm never publicly acknowledged for the contributions I've made to the lives of others, I'm satisfied with knowing that my reward is truly in the work. And my legacy lives on in the lives of each and every person I have inspired. Credited or not.

When onstage sharing insight and shedding light on matters that impact the lives, careers, and trajectories of people in the entertainment industry, I love to see the proverbial light bulbs turning on in the minds of those having an *aha* moment. Nothing has been more gratifying than sharing truths and practices that can help the next generation of young producers, actors, directors, singers, and entertainment professionals succeed. These are the moments I cling to, and the logs that keep the fire within burning on the coldest of nights. Thank you so much to every person who has ever attended and/or contributed to Hollywood Confidential over the last decade. Your support has anchored me through my toughest storms and served as a North Star in my darkest skies. I love each and every one of you, endlessly.

So now it's been established. I know, beyond the shadow of any doubt, that I have a powerful light that is shining in me, and I also know that part of my purpose is to shine that light in areas that are dark, so that others can find their way. And you do as well. As you continue to read these pages, I want to encourage you to think about your own luminosity—both the light that's shining in you and the lighthouse you can become for others. In these often dark times in which we live, your life, and the light within you, can be the reason that someone decides to continue to fight the good fight. To stay in the race. To not quit. To never give up. That's the type of life I want to lead, and the legacy I want to leave behind.

In the cosmos of Hollywood, few stars have shined brighter than Viola Davis. Winner of the coveted EGOT—as the recipient of an Emmy, Grammy, Oscar, and Tony award—Viola deserves *all* of her things.[1] I have had the esteemed honor and privilege to work with this Hollywood luminary not once but twice—most recently on the aforementioned WACO Gala special I sold to Oprah's network, in which Viola graciously spoke on the power of servicing underserved markets and marginalized communities. What I love about Viola and her story is that even through the darkest times, she never allowed her light to be extinguished. And when she rose to prominence, she used her light to spark a revolution that has been felt throughout the entertainment industry and the world at large.

Raised in Central Falls, Rhode Island, Viola has spoken publicly about what it was like to grow up in poverty conditions, at times enduring rat-infested apartments, long stints of no running water or electricity,[2] and even experiencing sexual abuse at a very young age.[3] As a form of escapism, she immersed herself in the world of theater and the arts. Following a six-week summer program at Circle in the Square Theatre in New York City,[4] Davis was encouraged to enroll in Juilliard, Yale, NYU, or the University of New York for their prestigious theater programs.[5] She wanted to apply to all four, but because she only had enough money for one application fee, she chose Juilliard. Viola was accepted and spent four years at the renowned performing arts conservatory, receiving her degree in fine arts.[6] After making her Broadway debut in *Seven Guitars*, August Wilson's Pulitzer-nominated play, in 1996, she received her first Tony for Best Actress in 2001 for her performance in *King Hedley II*.[7] Shortly thereafter, she appeared in the film *Doubt*, which brought her first Oscar nomination for Best Supporting Actress, paving the road for her second Oscar nomination for her role in *The Help*. Surprisingly, her two Oscar nominations didn't move the needle in her movie career. So she turned to television, accepting the lead role in Shonda Rhimes's *How to Get Away with Murder*, starring as Annalise Keating, a high-profile defense attorney and law professor. The show ran for six seasons. And in 2015, Davis became the first Black actress to receive an Emmy Award for Outstanding Lead Actress in a Drama Series.[8]

In this history-making moment, Viola would have had every right to center her acceptance speech on her achievements. Instead, she made a decision to shed light on racial inequalities, advocating for change in the industry on behalf of women of color everywhere, ensuring that they were at the forefront of the narrative. As her star has continued to rise, so has her passion for various humanitarian causes, including civil rights, women's issues, refugees,[9] sexual abuse, and ending childhood hunger.[10]

THE LIGHT
WITHIN YOU WAS
MADE TO SHINE.
LET. IT. *SHINE*.

Continuously choosing to leverage her fame to shed light on issues that impact the world is one of the most selfless acts I have witnessed in this industry. And in choosing to use the broken pieces of her life as fuel to ignite her star, her luminosity is at an all-time high, shining so brightly that it's blinding.

One of the most powerful and luminous forces within the entertainment industry, to date, Viola is the most Oscar-nominated Black actress in history, and the *only* Black actress with two Best Actress nominations.[11] Her life and accomplishments have become that of a shining star for all to see what our lives can truly be.

———

The light within you was made to shine. Let. It. *Shine*. You never know whose life you will inspire. Just like Viola, we can make a conscious decision to shine our light on injustices to do our part in helping to make the world a better place. I'm thankful for trailblazers like her, and my mentors from afar, John Singleton and Debbie Allen, who allowed their lights to shine through their gift for depicting, directing, and storytelling. It's what made me want to come to Los Angeles. Their light shined so brightly that it guided my path. And now I've used my light to help identify and inspire the next generation of dreamers. That's a lesson within itself. Wherever you are, and whatever you do, always remember that one of the most powerful ways to practice shining your light, and invest in the lives of others, is by sharing your own story. When we are intentional about sharing our stories in a way that uplifts and makes space for others, we are once again making deposits into our spiritual bank accounts, upon which one day we will make an undeniable withdrawal.

My friends, I hope you can see that this—investing in the lives of others—is exactly what I've been doing in these pages. Through sharing the lessons I've learned from some of the greats, I've given you the ingredients to formulate your very own version of success. And I'm not threatened by your success. I celebrate and I welcome it, as there is truly room for us all. I expect to see you winning in every aspect of your life. And if you ever happen to be in Los Angeles, and we're side by side— dining at Nobu, shopping at The Grove, or attending the Emmy, Grammy, or NAACP awards—let me know you practiced what you learned in these pages. I'm rooting for you. I see you. And I believe in you.

Shine.

And just like that, you've uncovered the twelfth and final secret within the formula of becoming the star of your own life.

FOUR WAYS

TO PRACTICE *LUMINOSITY*

BE A FORCE FOR GOOD

When we become a force for good, we commit to actions inspired by genuine concern for the well-being of others. We must learn to practice kindness, offer compassion, and seek to understand the emotions, experiences, and suffering of others. Empathy is the universal thread that has the power to unite humankind and light up our world. This week, even if it's just buying a sandwich for someone asking for money on the street, *be a force for good*.

SHARE YOUR STORY

Never underestimate the transformative power found within the art of storytelling. When we are transparent with others about our journey of self-discovery, the trials we've overcome, and even the battles we have lost, our story then becomes a beacon of light that can help guide others on their path to becoming their greatest self. Think of one person sharing a similar journey who could benefit from your story, and share it this week.

BE OF SERVICE

Being in service to others by committing to meet their needs is truly a light-bearing practice. Volunteering our time and resources to make a difference in someone's life instills a great sense of purpose and fulfillment in our own. In helping others, we in turn help ourselves, for, like a circle, whatever good we give out comes back to us. When we light a lamp for others, it brightens our path as well. This week, find one way to serve others.

ENTER INTO DIVINE AGREEMENT

When we get into divine agreement with our mission, our calling, and our purpose, the galaxy of stars within us begins to align in a way that causes us to radiate from the inside out, attracting experiences and opportunities that allow us to service our gifts in meaningful and impactful ways that help to evolve humanity. Life is a set of agreements, and by entering into the harmony and flow of our life's contract, we empower ourselves to perform on the world's stage as the star of our very own lives. Review the mission statement you've created, and confirm that you are living in agreement with your divine purpose.

QUESTIONS
for Reflection

Are there any internal issues or insecurities that have caused me to dim my own light?

What are the practical ways that I can stoke the light within me?

In what ways can I better platform my purpose on the world's stage? What opportunities do I seek?

How can I use my life to be a lighthouse to others? How can I show others the way?

Have I truly given myself permission to shine as the star of my own life? If I haven't, what needs to change?

AFFIRMATION
for Luminosity

THERE IS A BEAUTIFULLY BRILLIANT LIGHT LIVING within me—powerful enough to illuminate the darkest of nights, uncovering purpose's path. I embrace that light and accept my role as a lighthouse, fully permitting myself to shine luminously in the lead role as the star of my own life.

CONFIDENTIALLY . . .

I'm proud of you. Proud of you for being brave enough to take this journey of exploration and self-discovery with me. My hope is that you will walk away feeling empowered, equipped, and inspired to pursue the life of your dreams. Each of us has a unique set of deep-seated desires, hopes, and dreams embedded within the blueprint of our souls, but it is the relentless pursuit thereof that shifts those dreams into reality.

The final thought I will leave you with is that the world truly is a stage. And our experiences, circumstances, and the various roles people play in our lives—whether as heroines or as villains—are all intended for the expansion of our souls. We are all working together on the world's stage in a great ensemble cast to produce the best possible outcome for our individual and collective stories.

So today I ask you, are you living within the story you were made for? Are you starring in the life you were born to live? If the answer is no, and you don't like the way your story is unfolding, you don't have to stay stuck. As you implement these proven secrets for success, as the producer and author of your very own life, you have the power to pick up the pen of possibility and create the life you deserve as the lead character.

You see, to take our rightful place as the star of our own lives, we have to first be willing to accept that lead role on our life's stage. **That means no more co-starring, no more background acting, and no more hiding from the spotlight.** Your acceptance of this role means that you assume responsibility for your life. It means you begin, and continue, to make choices that align with your decision to be the best possible you that you can be. Once you've made that decision, once you've signed on the dotted line, once you're contractually obligated to take on the lead role in your own life, it's time to give yourself permission to shine.

It's time for you to shine.

Many of us have been taught that prioritizing our dreams and desires is selfish. But I vehemently disagree. I believe that prioritizing our purpose and well-being can be categorized as one of the greatest acts of love. I must first love myself before I can love and be of service to others. When we embrace this important act of radical love, we liberate ourselves— and those we encounter—granting them permission to shine. Conversely, when we refuse to platform our purpose, we betray ourselves, and others, becoming complicit in dimming our own light. And who has time for that? Not me. And certainly not you. At least not anymore.

So now that you know the secrets, be sure to let me know which chapter resonated with you the most! My hope is that these success stories, prompts, and affirmations have awakened the champion in you, allowing you to rise to every occasion victoriously.

As we wrap, I want to offer you a final charge and affirmation to keep you inspired on the journey to becoming the star of your very own life.

I pray that courage stretches out inside of you, and that optimism helps you see the invisible, feel the intangible, and achieve the impossible.

Never forget that you are a multifaceted, nuanced human being with many unique gifts to offer the world. May you believe in yourself like never before, allowing the light of faith to uncover your deepest truth and set you on your path to fulfillment. And even when obstacles threaten to deter you from achieving your goals, may ingenuity lead you to solutions that help you manifest the life you've always wanted.

But don't forget, if ever you feel too attached to a specific outcome, and things aren't going according to plan, you have the power to detach and let go. Surrendering to the flow of life always leads us to our highest good. Remember to be patient with yourself, as good things come to those who endure to the end. Even with that promise, you'll be met with challenges and negative circumstances in your life. In those moments, may you remember that in our darkest hours, we have the ability to shine our brightest.

Blessings and struggle are not mutually exclusive. And when you divorce yourself from that kind of binary thinking, you create space and opportunity for miracles to occur. Even the most beautiful opportunities will have challenges. But that's when you lean into your tenacity, daring to stare defeat in the face, declaring, "I will not lose!" And the truth is that when you couple that mindset with the practice of intentionality— homing in on your goals, identifying what you truly want out of life, and navigating how you will get there—you will always win.

So now, as you accept the lead role within your story, may authenticity be your guide, keeping you honest. Your star will always shine the brightest when you exercise the courage to be who you truly are. And above all, remember to never allow any circumstance, situation, person, place, or thing to dim your light. **Luminosity** is your portion. It is the fruit of your commitment to becoming the star of your own life.

In service,

ACKNOWLEDGMENTS

To God, the source of my strength and life—cowriting this book with You has been an absolute joy, and a dream come true. You are everything, and everything is You.

To my mother, Sheila Jones—your love and prayers surround me like a shield. The tremendous sacrifices you have made to enrich my life are immeasurable. And while I know there is no way I can pay you back, my plan is to show you that I understand. You are appreciated. I love you endlessly and am looking forward to our next and greatest chapter!

To my sister, Danyelle—thank you for being a mirror that has allowed me to fully see myself—the good, the bad, the great, and the flawed. May we continue to grow and work together in love to preserve and defend the Jones legacy. Also, thank you for making me an uncle! I love you, Olivia Elle.

To my good friend and bruv across the pond, Dr. Kumar Birch—thank you for teaching me the powerful tool of reframing, which has allowed me to find the good in everything, even that which is terribly bad. You are a true gift! Without you, this book would not have been possible.

To Walter Thomas and Carlos Patrick—I always wanted a brother, and now I have two in both of you. Thank you for your loyalty, advice, consistency, and prayers. I couldn't ask for better friends to walk through this journey with.

To Nicole Tossou—thank you for our "morning podcasts," which have helped ground me in an ever-changing world (and industry). Love doing life with you (and Jackson too).

To Dr. A. Pierre Sherrill II (and the EduLib consulting team), who helps me dot all the *i*'s and cross every *t* in life—so much love and appreciation. Thank you for everything you do for me.

To my Ohio State University family, with a special shout-out to Lester, Matt, David, Elijah, Monique M., Artina, Alisa, Monique F., Grace, and Vivian—thank you so much for always supporting my ideas and being patient through every ebb, flow, and iteration of me. The evolution continues, as does my love for each of you.

To Mr. Larry Williamson, the best director of D&I on the planet—what you did for generations of African American OSU alumni should be studied and implemented in institutions around the world. Forever grateful to you, Ms. Lee, Ms. Johnson, Ms. White, and the Frank W. Hale Black Cultural Center for fostering a tremendous sense of community, culture, and pride.

To every honoree who has ever touched our stage at Hollywood Confidential—thank you from the bottom of my heart. Your remarkable contributions to the evolution of humanity through sharing your art with the world have not gone unnoticed. You are seen, loved, valued, and appreciated.

To every soul who has ever attended an event or a workshop, or sent an encouraging word regarding our series—this book is my love letter back to you. Thank you for always showing up for me. Looking forward to another decade of making our dreams come true together. The marathon continues.

To the Harold Brothers, Ashley Richardson, Daniel Lee, Octavia Harper, Samantha Sims, Leo Wilson, Lamont Leak, Dunnie Onasanya, Miah Giavonni, Gene Cartier, Derrick A. King, Uriel Sanchez (the best photographer in the world), and every single person who has helped us produce our live activations at Hollywood Confidential—you are the unsung heroes of this operation, and without you guys, it wouldn't get done. Thank you.

To Rona Fourte, Orlena Blanchard, Sheereen Russell, Michelle Mitchell, Daniella Robinson, Anna Fuson, Kim Hardin, Kimberly Elise, Robi Reed, Ledisi, Mara Brock Akil, Tina Perry, Meagan Good, Fatima Elswify, Tracey Bell, Randi Matthews, Fatmata Kamara, and every incredible Black woman in my life—thank you for protecting me and speaking my name in rooms I haven't stepped foot in.

To Brandy—thank you for penning a beautiful foreword, and for being my North Star.

To Tabitha Brown—I am grateful to you for contributing to this project in so many wonderful ways. I sincerely appreciate your help and guidance. You are an angel.

A big shout to Brandon Hayes, Rishi Kumar, Jorge Torres, Aaron Bernard, A. J. Soares, Keith Collins, and James Morales—for helping with input on the creative, and for being a constant source of support during this entire process. And a huge thank-you goes to Jaimes Timas— for helping me come up with the idea for Hollywood Confidential. Your friendship and brotherhood have carried me through many seasons.

To Jennifer Smith and the entire team at SPIN—thank you for helping to make this dream a reality. And a very special thank-you to Danielle, Michael, and the HarperCollins/Celebrate family. Here's to a bestseller!

NOTES

INTRODUCTION

1. Stevie Mackey and Jennifer Lopez, "It's the Most Wonderful Time of the Year," YouTube, December 27, 2020, https://www.youtube.com /watch?v=7F7A2NRkwzg.

SECRET #1: COURAGE

1. Deb Sofield, "Leaving Greatness in the Graveyard," Deb Solfield, June 2023, https://debsofield.com/leaving-greatness-graveyard/.
2. Allison P. Davies, "Michael B. Jordan Will Be King," GQ, November 12, 2008, https://www.gq.com/story/michael-b-jordan-men-of-the -year-2018?_sp=5cf40340–1c87–4dce-a12f-d7e3772069a8.1727713120308
3. Craig Silverman, "New York Times Corrects Misquote of Thoreau's 'Quiet Desperation' Line," Poynter, April 30, 2012, https://www.poynter.org/reporting-editing/2012/new-york -times-corrects-misquote-of-thoreaus-quiet-desperation-line/.

SECRET #2: OPTIMISM

1. Oprah Winfrey and Marianne Williamson, "Oprah & Marianne Williamson: 20 Years After 'A Return to Love,'" Oprah.com, July 29, 2012, https://www.oprah.com/own-super-soul-sunday /oprah—marianne-williamson-20-years-after-a-return-to-love.
2. Brenda Alexander, "Brandy Recalls Meeting Whitney Houston 'At the Top' In Exclusive Audible 'Words + Music' Clip," Popculture, https:// popculture.com/music/news/brandy-recalls-meeting-whitney-houston -at-the-top-in-exclusive-audible-words-music-clip/.
3. BET, "Black Barbie 30th Anniversary," https://www.bet.com /photo-gallery/8bm7mv/black-barbie-30th-anniversary/2y8v4k.
4. "Brandy, Meagan Good, and Tichina Arnold Team Up for 'Hollywood Confidential' Event," September 2, 2014, YouTube, https://www.youtube.com/watch?v=hrKATINw8Rw.
5. Michael J. Fox, *No Time Like the Future: An Optimist Considers Mortality* (New York: Flatiron, 2020).

SECRET #3: NUANCE

1. Gary Trust, "This Week in Billboard Chart History: In 1999, Jennifer Lopez Jumped to Her First Hot 100 No. 1 with 'If You Had My Love,'" Billboard, June 10, 2019, https://www.billboard.com/pro/jennifer-lopez -if-you-had-my-love-this-week-in-billboard-chart-history-1999/.
2. Carlos Megía, "A Star Is Born or Made? How Jennifer Lopez Succeeded in Music Without Being a Good Singer," *El País*, July 22, 2023, https://english.elpais.com/culture/2023–07–22/a-star-is-born -or-made-how-jennifer-lopez-succeeded-in-music-without-being -a-good-singer.html#.

3. BMG, "INTL: Jennifer Lopez Global Superstar Signs New Recording and Publishing Partnership with BMG," September 12, 2023, https://www.bmg.com/de/news/Jennifer-Lopez-global-superstar -signs-new-recording-and-publishing-partnership-with-BMG.html.
4. Glenn Garner, "Jennifer Lopez Partners with Nonprofit to Deploy $14 Billion in Loan Capital to Latin Entrepreneurs," June 9, 2022, *People*, https://people.com/movies/jennifer-lopez-allocates-14-billion-latina -entrepreneurs-nonprofit-grameen-america/.
5. "JLO Adweek Speech" uploaded by Steve Jones, Dropbox, January 27, 2024, https://www.dropbox.com/scl/fi/98so6djyisfomfvxoqltz/JLO -ADWEEK-SPEECH.mp4?rlkey=s5ujb9vdijmd48i2tlavhp495&dl=0.
6. Coverage Book, https://app.coveragebook.com/215983 /books/f02a0aabfe8f53e2/sections/d5b7e7ae-f242–4907 -b9e8–16d58ef325ef?view=grid.

SECRET #4: FAITH

1. Steve Jones (@iamstevejones), "Party Over Here," Instagram, February 11, 2022, https://www.instagram.com/reel/CZ1__8_FUqH/.
2. CNN, "Showbiz Tonight" Transcripts, February 15, 2012, http://www.cnn.com/TRANSCRIPTS/1202/15/sbt.01.html.
3. Martin Luther King Jr., "Staircase," https://quoteinvestigator.com/2019/04/18/staircase/.
4. Lloyd Graham, "Blondin the Hero of Niagara," *American Heritage,* August 1958, https://www.americanheritage.com/blondin-hero-niagara.
5. Creative Bible Study, "The Charles Blondin Story," https://www.creativebiblestudy.com/Blondin-story.html.
6. Steve Persall, "The Secret Is Out . . . Angela Bassett Has Arrived," *Tampa*

Bay Times, June 25, 1993, https://www.tampabay.com/archive/1993/06/25
/the-secret-is-out-angela-bassett-has-arrived/.

7. Mandalit del Barco, "A Look Back at Oscar Nominee Angela
Bassett's Long, Distinguished Career," *NPR*, February 22, 2023,
https://www.npr.org/2023/02/22/1150988108/a-look-back-at-oscar
-nominee-angela-bassetts-long-distinguished-career.

8. del Barco.

SECRET #5: INGENUITY

1. Intersticia, "The Other 'I' Word—Ingenuity," March 25, 2020,
https://intersticia.org/the-other-i-word-ingenuity/.

2. Yasmin Gagne, "Issa Rae Talks Launching Her Own Prosecco
and Building a Creative Empire," *Fast Company,* October 18, 2023,
https://www.fastcompany.com/90969302/issa-rae-talks-hoorae
-viarae-prosecco-creative-empire.

3. "Issa Rae—Hollywood Confidential," YouTube, October 25, 2020,
https://www.youtube.com/watch?v=bq6NX2OfOI8.

SECRET #6: DETACHMENT

1. Claire Diab and Dennis Boyle, "The Seven Keys to Success—The
Sixth Principle: Detachment," Fire Engineering, May 9, 2013,
https://www.fireengineering.com/fire-life/the-seven-keys
-to-success-the-sixth-principle-detachment/#gref.

2. Sarah Regan, "Experts Explain What The Spiritual Law Of Detachment
Is + How To Use It," Mind Body Green, September 10, 2021,
https://www.mindbodygreen.com/articles/law-of-detachment.

3. Kennedy Center, "Oprah Winfrey," https://www.kennedy-center.org
/artists/w/wa-wn/oprah-winfrey/.
4. Jonathan Van Meter, "From the Archives: Oprah Winfrey in
Vogue," *Vogue*, May 25, 2011, https://www.vogue.com/article
/from-the-archives-oprah-winfrey-in-vogue.

SECRET #7: ENDURANCE

1. Monique Jones, "Golden Globes Nominees: Regina King Becomes Second
Black Woman to Get Best Director Nod," Blavity, February 4, 2021,
https://blavity.com/entertainment/golden-globes-nominees-regina-king
-becomes-second-black-woman-to-get-best-director-nod.
2. Regina King, interview by the author, Hollywood Confidential, Los
Angeles, October 7, 2017.
3. King.

SECRET #8: NEGATIVITY

1. T. D. Jakes (@BishopJakes), "You face the greatest opposition, when you're
the closest to your biggest miracle," X (formerly Twitter), September 10,
2015, 1:57 p.m., https://x.com/BishopJakes/status/642049266215686144.
2. David Ghiyam (@davidghiyam), "Someone speaking badly behind
your back? They take negativity away from your soul," Instagram,
September 22, 2023, https://www.instagram.com/reel/Cxg94WJJOFT
/?igsh=Y3pndWw0Y2N3aTVz.
3. Chuck Philips, "The Saga of Snoop Doggy Dog," *Los Angeles
Times*, November 7, 1993, https://www.latimes.com/local/la
-me-snoopphilips7nov0793-story.html.

4. Lortoume Hang'andu, "Snoop Dogg's Return to Jesus, Release of Gospel Album," God Reports, April 27, 2018, https://www.godreports.com/2018/04/snoop-dogg-returns -to-jesus-releases-gospel-album/.

5. Philips.

6. Philips.

7. Richard Harrington, "'Murder' Cashing in on Violence," *Washington Post*, November 1, 1994, https://www.washingtonpost.com /archive/lifestyle/1994/11/02/murder-cashing-in-on -violence/6cc116b8-e10c-4c5f-a8ac-852e27283718/.

8. Moritz Pommer, "Murder Was the Case," https://moritzpommer.com/murder-was-the-case.

SECRET #9: TENACITY

1. Tanza Loudenback, "The Incredible Rags-to-Riches Story of Starbucks Billionaire Howard Schultz," *Business Insider*, October 21, 2015, https://www.businessinsider.com/howard-schultz-profile-2015–10.

2. *Britannica*, "Saving Apple," https://www.britannica.com/mone y/Steve-Jobs/Saving-Apple.

3. Erica Hendry, "7 Epic Fails Brought to You by the Genius Mind of Thomas Edison," *Smithsonian Magazine*, November 20, 2013, https://www.smithsonianmag.com/innovation/7-epic-fails-brought-to -you-by-the-genius-mind-of-thomas-edison-180947786/.

4. Larry Shaffer, "You Really Can Learn as Much from Failure as You Do Success," *Fast Company,* June 19, 2022, https://www.fastcompany.com /90761446/you-really-can-learn-as-much-from-failure-as-you-do-success.

5. Gillian Telling, "How Tyler Perry Forgave His Abusive Father and Healed from His Traumatic Childhood," *People*, October 2, 2019, https://people.com/movies/how-tyler-perry-forgave-his-abusive-father-and-healed-from-his-traumatic-childhood/.

6. Oprah.com, "Tyler Perry's Traumatic Childhood," October 20, 2010, https://www.oprah.com/oprahshow/tyler-perry-discusses-being-molested-his-traumatic-childhood.

7. Jeremy Paul Gordon, "Inside Story: Tyler Perry and Oprah Bond over Painful Pasts," *People*, October 10, 2009, https://people.com/celebrity/inside-story-tyler-perry-and-oprah-bond-over-painful-pasts/.

8. Tyler Perry, "Tyler Perry's Story," https://tylerperry.com/tyler/story/.

SECRET #10: INTENTIONALITY

1. Ngozi Nwanji, "Beyoncé's Net Worth Reaches an Estimated $800M as Forbes Predicts She Is Well on Her Way to Becoming a Billionaire," Yahoo Finance, December 13, 2023, https://finance.yahoo.com/news/beyonc-net-worth-reaches-estimated-194145349.html.

2. Douglas Markowitz, "Afropop Legend Yemi Alade on New Album, 'Rebel Queen,' Historic Hits, & Working with Beyoncé," Grammy Awards, July 29, 2024, https://www.grammy.com/news/yemi-alade-interview-classic-hits-new-album-rebel-queen-beyonce.

3. Guillaume Vieira, "Destiny's Child Albums and Songs Sales," Chartmasters, July 19, 2022, https://chartmasters.org/destinys-child-albums-and-songs-sales/#albums_cspc_results.

4. Ethan Millman, "Beyoncé Just Became the First Black Artist with a Number One Country Song," *Rolling Stone*, February 20, 2024, https://www.rollingstone.com/music/music-country/beyonce-first-black-woman-number-one-country-song-texas-hold-em-1234970301/.

5. Alexandra Ilyashov, "Beyoncé Pulled the Biggest Power Play in *Vogue*," Refinery29, August 20, 2015, https://www.refinery29.com /en-us/2015/08/92660/beyonce-vogue-cover-story-no-interview.

6. *Harper's Bazaar*, "Beyoncé's Evolution," August 10, 2021, https://www.harpersbazaar.com/culture/features/a37039502 /beyonce-evolution-interview-2021/.

7. Bernadette Giacomazzo, "Beyoncé's Parkwood Entertainment Reportedly Generates $12M Annually—Here's How," Yahoo Finance, September 30, 2022, https://finance.yahoo.com/news/beyonc-parkwood-entertainment -reportedly-generates-170001094.html.

8. Lester Fabian Brathwaite, "Break My Soul, Break These Records: Beyoncé's Renaissance World Tour by the Numbers," *Entertainment Weekly*, October 3, 2023, https://ew.com/music/beyonce -renaissance-tour-by-the-numbers-records/.

SECRET #11: AUTHENTICITY

1. Jalen Rose, "Jalen Rose Cooks Up Conversation with Vegan Chef Tabitha Brown," *New York Post*, January 12, 2023, https://nypost.com/2023/01/12 /jalen-rose-talks-with-vegan-chef-tabitha-brown/.

2. Genesis Rivas, "Tabitha Brown Shares the Tips That Made Becoming Vegan Easy and Fun," *Shape*, April 18, 2022, https://www.shape.com /healthy-eating/diet-tips/tabitha-brown-tips-vegan-diet.

3. Michael Blackmon, "How a Vegan TikTok Star Became a Daily Pick-Me-Up for Millions of People," BuzzFeed News, April 21, 2020, https://www.buzzfeednews.com/article/michaelblackmon /tabitha-brown-vegan-tiktok-recipes-videos.

4. Ellen Degeneres, "Tabitha Brown Is Proof That Manifestation Is Real," Facebook, January 25, 2022, https://www.facebook.com/watch/?v =473963884238140.

5. Laverne Cox and Tabitha Brown, "Laverne Cox and Tabitha Brown Talk Being Yourself—Bonus Clip!" Let's Target, March 3, 2021, https://www.youtube.com/watch?v=Y3VXX0m3PLc.

6. Tabitha Brown (@iamtabithabrown), "The Video That Changed My Life 6 Years Ago," TikTok, December 30, 2023, https://www.tiktok.com /@iamtabithabrown/video/7318478125724126506?lang=en.

7. KC Ifeanyi, "How Tabitha Brown Is Building an Entertainment Empire Based on Joy," *Fast Company*, April 1, 2023, https://www.fastcompany.com/90873390/tabitha-brown -seen-loved-heard-entertainment-empire-joy.

8. Tabitha Brown, "Live from Hollywood Confidential in Beverly Hills," Facebook video, August 18, 2022, https://www.facebook.com/share/v /PXqntBLFsvtrC4MA/.

SECRET #12: LUMINOSITY

1. Siladitya Ray "Viola Davis Reaches EGOT Status, Here Are the 17 Others Who Have Achieved This Unique Honor," *Forbes*, February 6, 2023, https://www.forbes.com/sites/siladityaray/2023/02/06/viola-davis-reaches -egot-status-here-are-the-17-others-who-have-achieved-this -unique-honor/#.

2. John Lahr, "Viola Davis's Call to Adventure," *New Yorker*, December 11, 2016, https://www.newyorker.com/magazine/2016/12/19/viola-davis -call-to-adventure.

3. Mekishana Pierre, "'Finding Me': 8 Biggest Bombshells from Viola Davis' Memoir," ET Online, April 26, 2022, https://www.etonline.com/finding-me-8-biggest-bombshells-from-viola-davis-emotional-memoir-183053.

4. Jack Smart, "The Continued Education of Viola Davis and Denzel Washington," *Backstage*, updated July 23, 2020, https://www.backstage.com/magazine/article/continued-education-viola-davis-denzel-washington-5211/.

5. Viola Davis, *Finding Me* (New York: HarperOne, 2022).

6. *Juilliard Journal*, "Alums Take Home Emmys," October 2015, https://journal.juilliard.edu/journal/1509/alums-take-home-emmys.

7. Tony Awards, "Winners," 2010, https://www.tonyawards.com/winners/?q=viola.

8. Camila Domonoske, "Viola Davis Is First Black Woman to Win Emmy for Best Actress in a Drama," *NPR*, September 20, 2015, https://www.npr.org/sections/thetwo-way/2015/09/20/442084867/viola-davis-becomes-first-black-woman-to-win-emmy-for-best-actress-in-a-drama.

9. Viola Davis (@violadavis), Instagram reel, September 21, 2021, https://www.instagram.com/violadavis/reel/CUGae-_gOJ0/.

10. Sara Moniuszko, "Viola Davis Talks Protests, Diversity in Hollywood: 'I Feel Like My Entire Life Has Been a Protest,'" *USA Today*, July 14, 2020, https://www.usatoday.com/story/entertainment/celebrities/2020/07/14/viola-davis-talks-protests-diversity-media-vanity-fair-issue/5433829002/.

11. Joey Nolfi, "Viola Davis Makes Oscar History as the Most-Nominated Black Actress Ever," *Entertainment Weekly*, March 15, 2021, https://ew.com/awards/oscars/viola-davis-most-nominated-black-actress-oscar-nominations/#.

ABOUT THE AUTHOR

Transitioning from marketing projects like *Creed* and Quentin Tarantino's *Hateful Eight* into full-time TV production, Jones's notable executive producer credits include Jennifer Lopez's first holiday visual and Oprah Winfrey Network's Wearable Art Gala special featuring Tyler Perry, Viola Davis, and the first TV interview with Beyoncé in six years. He additionally produced three seasons of OWN's record-breaking No. 1 docuseries, *Black Love*. Jones also prides himself on being a trusted host and journalist, credited with landing the first interview with Ben Affleck and J.Lo as a reunited couple for *Adweek*. He also facilitates dynamic conversation with the likes of Oscar-winning Regina King, Angela Bassett, Lupita Nyong'o, Issa Rae, and more at his event series, Hollywood Confidential, a forum devoted to helping creatives of color break into the industry. An esteemed member of the Television Academy, Jones has been featured in *Variety*, *People*, and in *ESSENCE* magazine's Hollywood Issue for his impact on the industry. He's also appeared as a repeat guest on CNN shows *Anderson Cooper 360*, *CNN Tonight* with Don Lemon, and *ShowBiz Tonight* with AJ Hammer.